I.C.O.N.

I.C.O.N.

The Proven Blueprint to Build Credibility, Create Demand, and Stand Out in Any Market

Justin Heuff, Chad Durfee & Jared Zuckerman

Published by Game Changer Publishing

Paperback ISBN: 978-1-969372-20-9
Hardcover ISBN: 978-1-969372-21-6
Digital ISBN: 978-1-969372-22-3

GAME CHANGER
PUBLISHING

www.GameChangerPublishing.com

Read This First

Just to say thanks for buying and reading our book,
we'd love to invite you to join our ICON Community.

Scan the QR Code Here:

SCAN ME

I.C.O.N.

The Proven Blueprint to Build Credibility, Create Demand, and Stand Out in Any Market

JUSTIN HEUFF, CHAD DURFEE
& JARED ZUCKERMAN

Table of Contents

INTRODUCTION

The world around us is changing faster than at any time since the Industrial Revolution, and access to information through digital communities, tech, and even artificial intelligence is compounding that growth at a rate that hasn't been seen in all of human history. This is an incredibly exciting time to be alive, but this progress is also creating a harsh reality for most businesses and experts.

In today's content-saturated world, where people's attention spans are shorter than their toes, true expertise no longer wins—visibility does. In a world where people like Mr. Beast, Jake Paul, Kim Kardashian, and Andrew Tate, who have no industry expertise, are making tens of millions more than our Nobel Peace Prize winners, this reality is obvious, but it is happening at the micro level as well.

Are there other people in your industry who are providing the same services as you but who are much less skilled? Success is no longer about how good you are, but how visible you are. If the market doesn't see you outside of a LinkedIn profile, a website, and some Google reviews, they don't trust you.

This tidal wave of mediocre content is drowning the experts. Over the past five years, I've watched thousands of incredibly talented professionals struggle to grow their businesses, not because their funnel was broken, they hired the wrong marketing agency, or they were using the wrong strategy, but because they failed to stand out from the crowd. They assumed that their problems were tactical when, in reality, they were much deeper. The public perception of their industry credibility was too low.

Businesses that don't stand out in the right ways will always struggle to grow, no matter the strategy or tactic they use. The problem is how easily people can create mass content that distracts and blinds the market like a fog, hiding the real experts.

So, how do you stand out without having to mass-produce content and lose your sanity while doing it? You become the lighthouse. You leverage a few incredibly powerful strategic pieces of content that are more heavily weighted and will do more for your visibility than a thousand social media posts. You don't need to post three times a day, losing your privacy and sanity in an effort to put out more subpar content. You need to create strategic pieces of content that trigger the psychological drivers behind trust and authority.

In this book, we're going to show you what those drivers are and teach you the icon formula for implementation. You don't need to become an influencer; you need to become an icon. If you do this right, you can stop chasing clients, as the clients will come to you. You can stop competing on price and set your own. In the chapters ahead, we will lay out the framework for a proven formula that will help you engineer public perception of your authority, credibility, and expert status so that your name becomes synonymous with excellence in your industry.

"Icon" stands for industry credibility—that means establishing authority by creating signature pieces of content that work harder than a thousand posts could. An icon doesn't just read the book; they write it. They don't just appear as a guest on the podcast; they own the podcast. They don't just join the networking group; they create the group.

In the chapters ahead, you'll learn:

- How most businesses are unknowingly stuck in the **Invisible Expert Trap**

- The **psychological triggers** that shape public perception—and how you can activate them to your advantage

- The **key pieces of foundational content** that carry the most weight in influencing public perception, helping you work smarter, not harder

- How to become the **go-to expert in your field**—without becoming a dancing monkey on the stage of social media

By the end of this book, you'll have a practical, actionable plan to become an undeniable authority in your industry—a highly visible and deeply trusted expert—without sacrificing your voice or values through inauthentic content creation.

You might take a moment to google your name right now and screenshot the first two or three pages of results because, when you apply the principles in this book, those search results won't look the same ninety days from now. You'll see your name on podcasts, books, and stages, and what you'll notice are the new credibility signals that trigger the perception of expertise rather than invisibility. More importantly, your clients and industry partners will notice them, too. So, let's get to work and make you an icon in your industry!

PART 1

THE PSYCHOLOGY
OF ICON STATUS

CHAPTER 1

The Science of Celebrity & Why You Must Stand Out

Why People Work With Those They See the Most (Familiarity Bias)

"Familiarity bias" is a psychological phenomenon where people trust, prefer, or even like things they see more often. This is especially important in business because it often determines who gets the sale, referral, investment, or opportunity. The best experts are usually poorer than the best marketers because the best marketers understand how to grab the most valuable attention.

Studies have shown that people are 50 percent more likely to trust or develop a liking for something just by being exposed to it multiple times, and customers who see a person, brand, or company over multiple channels are 90 percent more likely to buy than they would be otherwise. That's why some of the top influencers in the world are also some of the wealthiest people, though they have no real skills or expertise.

Influencers such as Mr. Beast, the Paul Brothers, or the Kardashians have no real skill other than the ability to generate more attention than other people.

That increased their perceived status, and they turned that perceived status into money. They used that money to hire smart team members, who helped them grow their businesses exponentially.

This is called "the exposure effect," and studies have shown that people develop trust for things they see more often. They have no way of truly knowing who the best experts are, other than what they see online. The skewed perception of status, based on the content they can find online, is what drives people's decisions more often than not.

There lies the problem with invisibility. Nobody trusts you. If you are not willing to adapt and face the discomfort of growing your perceived status, you are going to continue to shrink as the world advances. We hear things like this all the time: "I don't want to be on social media because it feels inauthentic, and that's just not who I am," and "I don't need to do anything else because I work by referrals and I get them all the time." Well, the problem with that thought process is that you become increasingly invisible.

Maybe you have impostor syndrome and think, "I can't be an icon in my industry because I'm not a top expert," "I don't like to promote myself," "I don't have to do ego marketing," or any other excuse not to create status. If so, you will stay small—and while there is nothing inherently wrong with staying small, you might think otherwise when the next economic downturn hits and your limited leads dry up.

The most iconic individuals on the planet have never been the best experts. They've just been perceived as having the best expertise and being the ones most willing to put themselves out there. So, the major problem with being invisible is that your skill and expertise aren't enough anymore. If people don't see you as an authority, they don't trust you, and if they don't trust you, they don't work with you.

People are bombarded with content every day, and they don't have time to research too deeply, so what they see in a ten-second Google search can make or break their decision to engage with you. In an AI world that makes mediocre content creation easy, markets are saturated and competitive, and it is harder than ever to stand out. Luckily, there are foundational pieces of content you can create that will always put you in first place. The top icons engineer powerful visibility through key strategic pieces of content that score more influence points than others. Writing books, having podcasts, appearing on TV, and speaking in public create more perceived status and credibility than most other methods combined.

A great example of this is Robert Cialdini. Before he was known as a world-famous sales psychologist, he was just another professor. But then something happened: he wrote a book, and that book went global, and then everybody started quoting from it and mentioning it in their conversations. Before he knew it, Robert Cialdini was recognized as the world's foremost expert in sales psychology. Did that mean he was the top expert? No, and that didn't matter. Public perception is all that matters. He was sought after for his coaching programs, consulting services, and high-paying speaking engagements on stages around the world...all of which perpetuated his familiarity with people.

Now, salespeople and marketers alike think you are weird if you haven't heard his name or read one of his books. People assume, because he wrote a book on a few already well-known principles in psychology, that every professor in the world knows that he is the top expert in his industry. Many other psychologists are just as educated on those principles, and many, I'm sure, have more actual expertise in those areas than Cialdini, but because he wrote the book, he was the one who leveraged the familiarity bias to engineer social influence and gain massive trust at scale, and he has never looked back.

Proactive, strategic content is key. My formula for staying top of mind is **F.A.M.E.** The "F" stands for **frequent exposure** because people trust what they see most often. "A" stands for **association**, which means finding ways to be associated with other leaders and industry experts, such as by featuring them on your podcast, being a guest on their podcast, speaking alongside them on stages, being mentioned by them in endorsements, etc. "M" stands for **multi-channel omnipresence**, which means you are seen on multiple platforms and with foundational elements of icon status. That could be a book, social media videos, TV, a podcast, etc. "E" stands for **engagement in the market**. What types of content and platforms are currently being used to stand out, and how can you start using them? The lesson here is that the more people see you, the more they trust you, and the more they trust you, the more they want to work with you.

The Halo Effect—How Perception of Expertise Outweighs Actual Expertise

There's another cognitive bias at play here: "the halo effect." First identified in the 1920s, it was observed when officers rated soldiers they liked more as being more competent—even in areas completely unrelated to their actual performance. In other words, we assume that because somebody excels in one area, that must mean that they're great in other areas as well. So, if you excel in your area of expertise and you are the go-to person in your industry for that expertise, it's assumed that you're good in other areas, too.

This matters because most people will make snap judgments about who they want to work with, who they want to partner with, or whose network they want to be in based on their perception of reality rather than actual reality and credentials. Buyers, investors, and referral partners don't always have the time to look at every detail before they decide whether to work with you.

Instead, they will perceive your value based on what they can see or find out about you in a short period.

In this case, the perception of credibility is often much more influential than actual expertise or competence. If someone looks like an expert, acts like an expert, and is seen online as an expert, then we assume they're an expert, and usually, we do not take the time to verify it by looking at their actual credentials. Now, this is important because 56 percent of people rate somebody who's published a book as more credible and authoritative than somebody who hasn't, and 72 percent of people will judge a business or service provider's credibility based on content they can find online. This could be podcasts, news articles, or even a website that looks like it wasn't built in 2009.

There are even key psychological indicators or triggers that can initiate the halo effect in people. For example, a person wearing a lab coat is more likely to be trusted, even though they may not be a real doctor. In the same way, a great website design, book cover, or polished speaker reel might make you look like an expert as well.

We also tend to believe what other people believe, and this social proof is seen when people use testimonials, awards, media features, and other high-profile associations that trigger trust. All of these things trigger trust due to the halo effect, giving the impression that a particular person is trustworthy. Another example is that if somebody is constantly creating useful content, we automatically assume they're more knowledgeable, even if we don't read into it or find out where they're getting the content from.

The world we live in today isn't fair, but it is completely predictable, and people don't choose the best; they choose the best known. They don't trust the most experienced; they trust the most visible. Your mission, should you choose to accept it, is to look, sound, and appear iconic using strategic and intentionally designed foundational content to alter and influence the perception of the public until it becomes a reality. If you truly are the best expert in your space, not doing this is a disservice to the public, as it means you are leaving them to work with the people who are less talented and experienced but more apt to be trusted because of the content they're putting out, and you're not.

The "Top of Mind = Top of Market" Equation

One equation that I love is psychology + consistency = positioning power. It's not about being the best at what you do; it's about being the first name people remember when they need what you do. This is what I call the "top of mind, top of market equation." Being top of mind means that your name is the first one that comes up when somebody thinks about your niche or industry. If you are the first person somebody thinks of when they are looking for a leader or expert, even if you're not technically the most talented or skilled, it will still get you to the top of your market.

People make decisions based on what comes to mind the easiest, not always what's objectively better, and we tend to trust brands and people that we recognize, even subconsciously. There's something called the "mere exposure effect." Similar to familiarity bias, it says that the more somebody is exposed to you, the more they like and trust you, regardless of your actual performance.

As most marketers know, it takes five to seven brand impressions before somebody remembers your brand, but people are 90 percent more likely to convert when you hit those numbers. Consumers need to see you more often to trust you, and 70 percent of buying decisions are made before somebody even talks with a salesperson, meaning visibility does most of your selling.

If one of your clients refers you to a friend, you can't just rely on that referral to close like you used to twenty years ago. Before the internet, that referral was gold because the person had no choice but to trust the source. Now the referral is just the beginning. It's the entry point; it's their opportunity to go online and see if what they find matches the referral's explanation of why you're great. If what they find doesn't match, they probably won't meet or work with you. Even worse, if they can't find anything about you, which is typically worse than finding negative things, they likely won't even respond to the introduction.

Grant Cardone understood the "top of mind, top of market" equation well. Love him or hate him, you have to admit that he got one thing right early on: attention is currency. He committed to omnipresence by posting multiple videos a day, running ads, writing books, and doing every speaking engagement he could get, generating a massive social media presence.

He was not the most advanced sales trainer, and in fact, a lot of his sales training didn't work that well, but when you think of sales and the coaching and consulting space, his name is one of the first that comes to mind. That alone made him a hundred-million-dollar brand, and now he's one of the top influencers in his market because he always stays top of mind. Grant understood the death of invisibility and why creating an icon status could change everything.

Another good example of this is when you are in a Facebook group like ClickFunnels or another marketing group and somebody posts, "Hey, does anybody know a good [insert profession here]," and somebody's name gets tagged multiple times. That is somebody who is likely top of mind and putting themselves in a position of authority. Would anyone tag your name in those groups? Would they even think of you at all?

If you're not top of mind, you don't exist. If you are top of mind, you'll get more referrals without even having to ask because people will trust you faster. This will attract more opportunities like speaking engagements, media opportunities, and partnerships, and you will become the default, which means less friction in every area of your business.

Again, people don't always choose the best option; they choose the most familiar, trusted, and accessible option. Your digital presence is your resume. Would you apply for your dream job without a resume, or would you make that baby the nicest, most complete, and most compelling thing ever? You need to think about your social status in the same way. If somebody googles you and finds nothing of value, you're not top of mind; you're invisible. Or if there is some value, but it's difficult to access and find because it's on page two or three of Google, again, you're invisible.

The purpose of this book is to orchestrate the death of your invisibility so you can dominate your market. Now would be a good time to do a good self-audit. Google your name, and what shows up? Would you work with yourself? Would you hire yourself? Would you trust yourself? Don't be the best-kept secret in your space. Being amazing in the shadows is business suicide because the market does not reward talent; it rewards visibility.

Just as the squeaky wheel gets the grease, the loud expert gets the attention. In a world more and more addicted to scrolling and swiping, where names are buried beneath hashtags and highlight reels, the one who is seen the most becomes the one who wins the most, not because they're better or more talented, but because they're top of mind. In the end, that's all business is: a game of memory. Stay top of mind so you can stay on top of the market.

CHAPTER 2

The Status Economy: Social Capital, Perception, and Authority

Why Social Capital is the New Currency of Business Success

I want to talk about social capital and why it is the new currency of business success. Besides the will to survive, the next deepest human motivator is the will to matter. The desire, the need even, to be wanted, to feel important, to feel desired, is one of the deepest human motivators and is built into our DNA. In caveman days, if you were kicked out of your tribe, it would be a death sentence. We are wired to survive, and we inherently understand that social capital is vital to our survival as a species.

Human capital is your knowledge, skills, and experience. Financial capital is your money and assets. Social capital is your influence, connections, and credibility within your network. In this new age of tech and AI, people are finding it harder than ever to distinguish between what is real and what is computer-generated. We no longer know if the copy we see on the sales page, the voice we hear on the phone, or the video we watch on YouTube is human or not. As a result, we are striving for more human connection than ever, and relying on our trust in our networks.

We experience **three main types of social capital** in our networks, and we need to focus on all three equally:

1. **Bonding capital** – This consists of the deep trust we have within our inner circles, such as clients, referral partners, family, and friends.

2. **Bridging capital** – These are important connections that link us to new people, industries, and opportunities. Examples include podcast hosts, LinkedIn connections, and members of other digital communities.

3. **Linking capital** – This refers to special connections with the power and influence to connect us with larger communities. These might include media outlets, high-level leaders, celebrities, investors, and influencers.

According to an article by Tristan Claridge from Social Capital Research & Training, most people invest 80 percent of their time in bonding capital and never grow beyond their comfort zone to focus on bridging and linking capital within their networks. You need all three to become an icon. You can use your social capital to invest in network equity, which is your reputation and influence within your networks. Icons don't just have large networks— they're usually the center of gravity within those networks, and they've enriched and learned how to leverage all three types of social capital.

If you were to message your network and ask for ten referrals to new potential clients today, do you have enough bonding capital with members of your network to get those introductions? If you messaged your network to ask for a connection to a new joint venture partner or celebrity, do you have enough linking capital in your network to make that happen—or do you even have the right network? In this new world of tech and digital communities, our networks are more interconnected than at any time in human history. If you messaged your network and asked them to plug you into other large and high-value networks, do you have enough bridging capital for them to do that for you?

You may have heard that "your network is your net worth." When you gain fame, celebrity, influence, and icon status, you gain social favors, and those favors can turn into all kinds of material things. That "your network is your net worth" is still true today, but not as true as it was twenty years ago. If you haven't written any books, don't have a podcast, don't have much video content, and don't have much influence, your business is dying.

However, people like Gary Vaynerchuk, Grant Cardone, Tony Robbins, Mel Robbins, Joe Rogan, or any A-list celebrity, business titan, or Olympic athlete all have incredibly high-value networks, and they can leverage them in massive ways because people naturally want to be associated with them. Just as in caveman days, when you wanted to befriend the tribal chief, in modern days, you want to befriend the people who have the biggest social status because they are perceived as the most important.

Now, I want to make a distinction here. I'm not saying that because you don't have social status and aren't a celebrity that you're not important. That's the opposite of what I'm saying. Experts typically go broke, while marketers who have subpar offers typically make millions. They just understand that the more eyeballs they get and the higher their perceived value, the more money they make.

As human beings, our perception of the world, which has been built by our upbringing, childhood, familial connections, friendships, and experiences, is our reality. Perception is reality. So, what we want to do is build the perception of status and importance by putting together foundational pieces of content and making strategic moves online. The goal is that people perceive you as an icon in your industry, as the best. When they do, they're going to want to be in your network, work with you, and refer you.

This is not an ethical conundrum; it is just an understanding of human psychology and a willingness to work with it, rather than fight against it. I hear people all the time say, "I don't want to be online. I don't want to put my personal life out there for everyone to see. I don't want to have a social media following because it feels inauthentic." I understand that.

However, if you are invisible in today's day and age, you are untrustworthy. If people can't see you, hear you, watch you, or find anything that tells them that you're the best, they will not trust that you can do the job. They've been taken advantage of too many times, so the people they see working with the most people and with the highest net worth are the ones they want to work with, associate with, and refer to others.

Are you a good investment for other people's social capital right now? If I were to google your name, what would I find, or even worse, what would I not find, that could quickly convince me you are a good investment of my time, finances, and social capital? Social capital is the new currency of business, so don't be P.O.O.R., "passing over opportunities repeatedly," to become an industry icon.

The Referral Paradox—Why Old-World Referrals No Longer Work

I want to take a moment to talk about referrals. It's often assumed that your network is your net worth and that people will naturally refer others to you just because they are in your network. That is no longer the case. The old-world referrals are dying, and what has replaced them is a new age of technology, artificial intelligence, and digital communities, where status celebrities and icons are more likely to get people to refer to you than not.

Before the internet, the Better Business Bureau, and Google reviews, a referral was ironclad and trusted. People had no choice but to trust a referral from a trusted friend. However, nowadays, when a client refers someone to you, the prospect will research you long before they meet with you, maybe even before they respond to you. What they find online—or even worse, what they don't find online, because, remember, if they can't see you, hear you, or listen to you, they won't trust you—makes all the difference. They are more likely to work with the person who has more social status and perceived expertise online in your industry.

Also, when people refer others, they are making a large investment in social capital and taking a major risk. If I were to refer somebody to the Mexican restaurant down the street and I told them that I had the best nachos of my life there, and then they went to that restaurant and had a bad experience, it's no big deal. They might lose $20, but it's not going to impact our relationship. They might just give me a hard time and make a fun joke about it.

However, if I refer somebody to a divorce attorney, whom they pay $100,000 and still end up losing their house, kids, car, and belongings, and go into a deep state of depression because of it, that might not only impact our lifelong relationship, but it could get around my social circles and digital communities and hurt my social capital.

This is especially true if that person finds out that I was paid a referral commission by that divorce attorney and turns them into a cheap paycheck instead of the relationship that they thought we had. That will not only ruin that relationship, but it will also 100 percent get around the rest of my network, decreasing the value of my role in it.

So, understand that when people refer others to you, they are taking a massive risk of potentially losing social capital if the experience doesn't go

JUSTIN HEUFF, CHAD DURFEE & JARED ZUCKERMAN

well. If you have a high-ticket offer or service, people are much less likely to refer others to you unless you can prove to them that you are a great investment in their social capital.

Just doing a good job with them isn't enough anymore. They need to see that you are an industry icon, the go-to expert in your space for what you do. They need to see that you've written a book, have a podcast, created a certification or award, spoken on stages, and so forth. When they do, they'll perceive you as an incredible investment in their social capital because, regardless of the experience their friend might have with you, they can always go back to "this person wrote a book on this topic" or "this person speaks on stages."

The higher your perceived value online and in content, not just any content, but foundational trust pieces, the more quantity and quality of referrals you will receive, and the more opportunities you will get. For more information on this, feel free to check out our other book, *The Referral Revolution*, where we go into the death of the old world of referrals and the emergence of a new world of referrals, and why you'll get left behind if you don't understand what no longer works.

The Invisible Expert Trap—Why Even Great Professionals Get Ignored

Imagine that you're a highly skilled expert. Your clients love you and your work, and you've invested years in your craft. You are so proud and truly believe that you might be the best of the best at what you do, but your business isn't growing. You're not getting the high-quality leads that you would like, and your network is stale. Meanwhile, you see people with half your skill set who are dominating your industry and getting media attention, speaking gigs, and high-ticket clients while on autopilot.

The invisible expert trap is when you rely too heavily on your expertise, certificates, title, and five-star reviews. Meanwhile, your competitors, who are not nearly as experienced or talented, are dominating your space because people know who they are. The world is not designed to find you; it's your job to be found.

You may remember the movie *Field of Dreams*, where a mysterious voice whispers to Kevin Costner over and over, "If you build it, they will come." I think a lot of entrepreneurs and experts alike have a romanticized idea of how this world works. You can build it, but they won't come unless you are top of mind and iconic in your industry.

Most experts make **three major mistakes** in their marketing efforts:

1. **Chasing vanity metrics**

    They obsess over how many social media likes they get or how many five-star reviews they have, rather than focusing on foundational and strategic content pillars that carry much more weight when it comes to trust and credibility. It doesn't matter how much content you post on social media if nobody can find your platforms or has a compelling reason to visit them.

2. **Using outdated marketing tactics**

    This includes having a website that looks like it was built in 2009, relying on generic SEO blogs stuffed with keywords, and sending cold, robotic email funnels. Even traditional one-to-one referrals can be considered outdated in today's world of tech, AI, and digital communities. These methods don't convey true credibility or establish a sense of authority and influence.

3. **Failing to stand out from the crowd**

We run three lead-generation companies and have worked with thousands of clients. One of the biggest challenges businesses face is consistently generating leads and acquiring clients. Many hop from marketing company to marketing company, from strategy to strategy—always chasing the next shiny object—yet continue to see mediocre or subpar results.

I propose that there is a deeper problem that 95 percent of businesses are experiencing in this new age of marketing. The clients and companies that had, by far, the most success with our lead generation tactics, and there are lots of different ones that we employ, were the ones that were perceived as being industry icons. If you were to search their names, every hit on the first, second, and third pages of Google would be about their companies. They've written books, spoken on stages, run podcasts, created awards and certifications for their industry, along with major masterminds and marketing events for members of their community, and are seen in the press as leading the way in their industry.

No matter what tactic they try, they find success, while other, less-known businesses struggle to find a single strategy that will work. The problem is not their client acquisition efforts; that is just a symptom. The root problem is that they don't stand out from the crowd.

Someone once asked me to imagine a field with a thousand elephants in it. They said, "If you were in that field as one of those thousand elephants, how would you stand out from every other elephant?"

I thought about that for a while and couldn't come up with an answer other than to say, "I would try to come to the front, jump, or do something different from the crowd."

The answer that was given to me was: "If you painted yourself pink, you would stand out from the rest." To this day, that answer gives me a strong visual. For a company to find success in anything, it needs to be the pink elephant in its industry.

There are a number of ways that you can do that, many of which we've discussed in this book, but here's the strategy in a nutshell:

- Don't read the book—write the book.
- Don't listen to the podcast—create your own podcast.
- Don't listen to the speaker at the event—be the speaker at the event.
- Don't just attend the mastermind—create your mastermind.
- Don't just accept the award—create your own award that you can give to other members of your industry.

To be the pink elephant, you need to own the platform. This is important because 90 percent of buying decisions are made subconsciously, and they are based on perception, not logic. Also, according to a 2020 report from industry-leading fintech company Ignite Sales, 70 percent of sales are influenced by a brand's perceived authority and visibility, while 67 percent of buyers say they trust the brands and companies they see frequently over those they don't.

Here are some examples of experts who escaped the trap and how they did it. We worked with a brilliant CPA who, like most CPAs, struggled to get consistent clients and grow. We helped him write a book and launch a niche podcast where he interviewed startup founders on finance challenges they were having. Within twelve months, he became the go-to financial advisor in that niche, and his business grew fivefold.

Another was a health and fitness coach who had a master's degree and raving client reviews, but had been in her industry for over ten years and couldn't break ten thousand a month. We helped her write her book, launch a podcast, and get herself booked at local speaking events. She recorded herself on stage and then turned those appearances into branded YouTube videos and Instagram shorts.

Within six months, she was inviting some of the biggest referral partners in her space onto her podcast, where she interviewed, highlighted, and acknowledged them, making friends and gaining reciprocity. At the end of the interview, she would give them a signed copy of her book, mention that she thought there might be a great referral partnership there, and ask them if they would like to discuss that further in another meeting. She closed over thirty new referral partners in the first sixty days, and now will never have to worry about gaining business again.

So, if you are going to escape the expert trap, you need to shift from expert to authority and not just be seen as good, but as the best. Write a book, speak on stages, start a podcast, get featured in major press, and document all of it to post online.

One of the biggest issues is that people think that presenting themselves as an expert for the world to see is an ego play. I hear all the time that it feels inauthentic and that they don't need that type of ego boost. I want to give those of you who feel that way a paradigm shift. Invisibility is not humility; it's sabotage. You don't serve more people by staying silent; you serve them by being seen.

PART 2

THE ICON METHOD—HOW TO BECOME THE MOST RECOGNIZED NAME IN YOUR INDUSTRY

CHAPTER 3

The Book—Your Crown Jewel of Authority

Why Every Industry Leader Has a Book, and the Author vs. Authority Principle

A book isn't just a collection of words or a bunch of sentences. Nowadays, it's a symbol of expertise, authority, and powerful marketing positioning. In the ever-increasingly crowded marketplace, a published book is still one of the most powerful ways to establish credibility, increase visibility, and earn public trust rapidly. A book is seen as the crown jewel of your authority, and everything else that you talk about can flow from there. It provides tangible proof that you know your topic, have found your thinking around it, and have something worth saying to the world.

The fact is, people probably won't even read your entire book. They may not even read any of your book, but the very fact that you have a book gives them the perception that you are a leader in your industry. That's what we are after: perceived influence, perceived expertise, and perceived iconic status. As we know, a person's perception is a person's reality.

Even in this digital age, with the explosion of video social media and AI-generated content, books still hold a unique psychological positioning. They carry a heavier weight than any other type of content you can produce. This is due to perceived effort, legacy signal, and status anchoring. Writing a book is still seen as difficult, and effort equals authority in most people's perception. Books are permanent and prestigious, and they still hold heavy intellectual weight, so legacy signaling also gives the perception of authority. And finally, being a published author still subconsciously places you in a higher professional tier than any of your competitors, and that status anchoring sets you apart from the crowd.

Books are still incredibly difficult to write and even more difficult to make valuable, and most people still don't give the time or effort or even have the expertise to be able to put words to paper in a way that is impactful enough to set them apart as authoritative figures and leaders in their industry. In the 2024 *Publish & Prosper* podcast, Lauren Vassallo and Matt Briel discussed that 94 percent of people surveyed said that publishing a book helped them establish their authority faster than anything else. And here's the kicker when it comes to being at the top of the mind economy: books are ten times more likely to be remembered than any blog content, YouTube videos, or social media posts.

As an example, Simon Sinek built a global brand just by publishing one book. You may have seen his TEDx talk "Start with Why," but that didn't start as a movement; it started as a concept, and that concept became a talk, which then became a book, and that book created a global phenomenon for businesses worldwide. The book gave the idea form and permanence, and it legitimized his expertise. Had it just been his TED talk, he still would have had more authority than not, but the book cemented his status as an icon in his space.

Just imagine for a moment that you're a salesperson, and you're looking to get a job with some of the biggest companies in the world. How do you stand out from all of your competitors, who are also amazing salespeople? Are they going to care that you received sales training from Brian Tracy, Grant Cardone, Jordan Belfort, or Jeremy Minor? Are they going to care how many millions of dollars you've closed in business?

Of course, they will, but how many of your competitors have written their own books on sales? This is where authority plays its role. If that company sees that you've not only read the books on sales but you've also written a book on the subject, it immediately sets you apart from the crowd and helps you stand out in a memorable and authoritative way.

There's something I like to call the "author versus authority effect." "Author" is the root word of authority, so becoming an author positions you as the originator of ideas and the authority around those ideas, not just another service provider. This is why nearly every industry leader has a book. Tony Robbins wrote *Awaken the Giant Within*, Brené Brown wrote *Dare to Lead*, Dan Sullivan co-authored *Who Not How*, Alex Hormozi wrote *$100M Offers*, Donald Miller wrote *Building a StoryBrand*, and the list goes on and on. The people who stand out from the crowd are the authority figures (i.e., the author figures).

Here's the number one excuse that keeps most business professionals and experts stuck: the idea that you're not ready to write a book yet. Are you teaching your expertise? Are you positioning yourself in your expertise? Are you emailing and explaining things about your expertise? Then you don't need more content or expertise; you just need a new structure, and a book is a refined structure of what you already know.

You don't write a book because you're an expert; you write a book because people need to know you're the expert. Imagine being a guest on somebody's podcast and, at the end, they give you a signed copy of their book. Do you look at it and immediately consider them an expert in that field? Of course, you do, and you do it without even thinking twice about it.

So, I'm going to challenge you at this point. If you've been in your field for three or more years and you haven't written a book yet, now is the time.

How to Write a Book in 90 Days (Even if You're Not a Writer)

Now that you know the importance of writing a book, let's talk about how you can do it in the next 90 days. You don't need to be a writer; you just need to have a good process. Writing a book is not about literary perfection; it's about the ability to clearly structure the expertise that is in your brain.

Before we get started, I want to address **three common misconceptions** that stop most people from writing a book. While 81 percent of Americans say they want to write a book at some point, only 3 percent ever do. Here's why:

- **Misconception #1: "I'm not a writer."**
  Most bestselling authors you see have had ghostwriters, editors, or dictation support. Their expertise and ideas are solid—but professionals help shape those ideas into content that's easy to read, follow, and feel inspired by.

- **Misconception #2: "I don't have time."**
  You can write for just 30 minutes a day and finish a book in 90 days. I've personally written a book in under four hours with the right tools and structure. In just 1 percent of your year, you can create an asset that supports your business and relationships for a lifetime.

- **Misconception #3: "I don't know where to start."**
  That's exactly what this chapter is for. It's your roadmap to get started and confidently publish your authority.

Step-by-Step Framework: Weeks 1–2

If I were to give you a simple step-by-step framework, I would say that weeks 1 and 2 should be saved for planning and positioning in your book, defining your core message or what you want your readers to learn, believe, and understand about something, the major paradigm shifts that you want to impart, the major beliefs that you want people to change, and more. You should have a very clear outcome for the purpose of your book and what the readers will achieve or get if they decide to read it.

The next step would be to speak it out using voice dictation and do what I call a book brain dump or storyboard, where you just talk to yourself and your computer about all the elements of your book.

Week 3

Week 3 involves structuring the book based on the content you dictated. A good example is dropping the content into ChatGPT and asking it to help you create an effective structure. Then, you make final edits to ensure that the structure fits the flow and design of the book you are writing.

Weeks 4–6

In weeks 4 through 6, you would create the first draft and follow the same process as you did in the brain dump, just talking out each chapter, each subsection of each chapter, and then going back and editing your words.

From here, you would start to consider any personal stories or anecdotes you know, find statistics and data that back up the positioning of your opinions and ideas, make sure to cite the sources so as not to plagiarize anything, and then begin to build the book.

The goal here would be to get a book that's somewhere in the range of twelve to twenty chapters and anywhere from four to seven pages per chapter. So, use the talk-it-out method for every chapter just to pull the expertise out of your brain, and then go back and edit it on paper so that you can put the content in a concise, understandable format.

Weeks 7–8

In weeks 7 and 8, I might use tools like Atticus, Scribner, or Vellum for formatting, or even better, I would hire a professional editor to go through and help me polish the book. I would also find a cover designer who could help me put together something visually compelling. You can also use Photoshop or Canva Pro if you want to do this yourself.

Weeks 9–12

Then, finally, in weeks 9 through 12, you get to publish and promote your book. You can self-publish on Amazon KDP or IngramSpark, or you can choose a paperback or hardback version of your book, or put it in audiobook format. Then tease the launch to your network so that they know it's coming, and you can leverage your bridging and linking social capital that we spoke about previously to get their support in getting your book out to the world.

To recap the book-writing framework in an organized step-by-step:

Weeks 1–2: Planning & Positioning

- Define your **core message** and what you want readers to:
  - Learn
  - Believe
  - Understand

- Identify major **paradigm shifts** and beliefs you want to challenge or change.

- Clarify the **outcome** of your book — what readers will gain by reading it.

- Establish your book's **purpose and transformation promise.**

Week 3: Brain Dump & Structuring

- Use **voice dictation** to create a "book brain dump" or **storyboard**:
  - Talk freely through your ideas and chapters.

- Drop your content into **ChatGPT** (or a similar tool) to help organize and structure it.

- Review and **finalize your structure**, adjusting the flow to fit your vision.

Weeks 4–6: First Draft Development

- Begin writing your **first draft** using the same voice-dictation method:
  - Speak through each chapter and subsection.

- o Transcribe, then **edit your own words** for clarity and tone.

- Start layering in:
  - o **Personal stories** or anecdotes
  - o **Statistics and data** to back your ideas
  - o Proper **citations** to avoid plagiarism

- Begin shaping the actual **manuscript**.

Weeks 7–8: Editing & Formatting

- Use tools like **Atticus, Scrivener, or Vellum** for formatting.

- Hire a **professional editor** to refine and polish your manuscript.

- Work with a **cover designer** to create a visually compelling book cover, or use tools like **Canva Pro or Photoshop** if you're doing it yourself.

Weeks 9–12: Publishing & Promotion

- Choose your publishing path:
  - o **Amazon KDP, IngramSpark**, or other platforms
  - o Decide between **paperback, hardback, and audiobook** formats

- Begin your **book launch strategy**:
  - o Tease the release to your **network**
  - o Leverage your **bridging and linking social capital** to spread the word and boost visibility
  - o Create a **marketing plan** to build momentum before and after launch

Use this book as the crown jewel of all of your marketing moving forward. As long as the ideas, expertise, and stories are your own, you can speak out your book as well. By following this process, you'll likely find that you have way too much information rather than too little, and you'll probably end up having to take out sections to improve readability.

For example, you may be familiar with the book *Atomic Habits* by James Clear. In its first version, it was over 120,000 words. Clear cut it in half after his editor called the original version bloated and confusing. But by putting all of his expertise, ideas, and stories into words on paper and then fine-tuning and cutting out any fluff, he was able to create a best-selling book that sold over ten million copies worldwide. Your rough draft is not meant to be pretty; it's meant to create structure, and then from there, you can chisel away at the sculpture until you've created your personal masterpiece.

Some of the tools that I would recommend if you're going to be doing this or starting the process on your own, for the outline, are Google Docs or Trello. For transcription, you could use Otter.ai or Descript. For editing and writing, you could use Grammarly, Hemingway Editor, or Google Docs. For formatting your book, you could use Atticus, Reedsy, or Scrivener. For publishing your book, you can use Amazon KDP or IngramSpark, and for designing the cover, you could use 99designs, Canva Pro, or Fiverr.

My suggestion would be to storyboard it, brain dump it, structure the chapters, and then speak out the rough version of it with a voice transcriber. Then find a reputable company, lean on their expertise, and work with them to chisel it down into your masterpiece. You don't have to be a writer; you just have to be somebody with something important to say, and as far as books are concerned, done is better than perfect. Remember, we're not striving for maximum readership; we're striving for maximum perceived authority, expertise, and icon status in your industry.

CHAPTER 4

The Podcast—Your Platform for Influence & Strategic Relationships

The guest strategy—Why starting a podcast connects you to power players

If writing a book is the crown jewel of your authority, the next closest thing would be starting a podcast. Starting a podcast isn't just about talking into a microphone; it's about creating a platform that gives you a reason to start conversations with influential people. A podcast isn't just content; it's a relationship-building machine.

One of the fastest ways to get the perception of authority is to borrow it, and when you start a podcast and invite other experts, industry leaders, influencers, potential referral partners, and power players as guests and give them a chance to talk about themselves, promote their work, and relay their ideas and expertise, you not only get to borrow their credibility and reach to increase your icon status, but you also get to build the net worth of your network by increasing the quality of the people in it.

Being the host puts you in control of the relationship, the narrative, and the platform, something that I call the "guest strategy." Growth doesn't necessarily happen from just talking on your podcast; it comes from inviting the right people onto your podcast. Whether the intention is to get new referral partners, new clients, more interesting content, or a higher-value network, it all leads to the same endpoint, which is icon status in your industry.

One of the reasons this works so well is that people love to talk about themselves, no matter who they are. All you are doing is giving them a platform that makes them feel like an expert, where they can promote their brand, book, or expertise. You give them what they want and need, which is content that they can use to promote their status socially.

By having guests on your podcast, you're building reciprocity by giving them a platform. On the back end, you're not asking for anything other than a partnership and borrowed credibility through the "proximity effect," which is being in close proximity and perceived friendship with other important people in the industry. You don't need a big platform or millions of downloads every month to invite these people onto your show; you just need to create the platform and the topic that you know they would love to talk about.

Over 464 million people listen to podcasts globally, and 54 percent of listeners are more likely to consider working with a brand that they hear about on a podcast. Over 90 percent of podcasts are hosted by people who have fewer than a thousand listeners per episode, but they still have incredibly high-value networks.

If you were to reach out to somebody and say, "I would love to talk to you about how you can join as a referral partner of mine and start sending me business," but they had no idea who you were, and what they saw or found about you online was minimal, do you think they would take that conversation seriously? Or would it go over smoother if you reached out to offer them something of value before making an ask, like a referral partnership, and invited them to be a guest on your podcast, already knowing that the theme, topic, and content of your show, even the title of your show, would be something that would resonate with them?

They will probably research you, and if what they find about you online is that you're an author, you have lots of content, and you are perceived as an icon in your industry, they are going to want to be a guest on your show. It doesn't mean you have to be an actual icon in your industry, but they need to perceive you as a valuable connection and possible addition to their network, and they need to see your platform, i.e., your podcast, as a valuable asset to their message.

Then, after interviewing, highlighting, and acknowledging them, when the podcast interview is over, you can say, "That was a great interview. I love what you're doing. You know, as you were speaking there, it dawned on me that there might be a great referral opportunity here between our two companies. I would love to chat with you about that on another call. Do you have any space tomorrow or the next day so I can talk to you about what I'm seeing?" Wouldn't that be a better way to land a new referral partner? Of course, it is, and we average ten to twenty new referral partners per month in our companies doing exactly this.

At the end of that podcast, you could also invite them into your network, to write a guest chapter in your book, to give an endorsement of your book, platform, or event, or to speak at your event. You could ask them for almost anything you wanted, and they would feel the need to reciprocate because you gave them a platform. You engaged reciprocity, and now they feel indebted socially, and you have a lot more power in this position.

The only thing I would recommend that you don't do on the back end of your podcast is try to sell them on your products and services, as that would cheapen the relationship, and it would be obvious that the reason you invited them onto the podcast was to try to sell them something. That feels bait-and-switchy and is never going to go over positively in the long run.

I would think of your podcast as a Trojan Horse. It's a gift on the outside, and on the inside, there's an intention behind it. It's not a bad or selfish intention, just a calculated intention to increase your perceived status by partnering with the right people, adding the right people to your network, and asking the right people to speak at your events and in your digital communities, giving you opportunities to access their networks at the same time. It should be a symbiotic relationship.

In a world that is saturated with cold pitches and cold content, inviting somebody onto a platform that you created and hosted is a great way to stand out from the crowd. So, if you're considering starting a podcast, here's how I would go about it. I would not just think of it as talking about something I want to talk about. If you want to create your own *The Joe Rogan Experience*, that's perfectly fine, but if you're doing this for social status and to stand out from the crowd, you need to understand what is going to do that the most.

Identify who the best potential referral partners for your company would be, who the best potential additions to your network would be, who the best potential speakers on your stages would be, who the best potential endorsements in your new books would be, and then start reaching out to these people to invite them to talk about their expertise on a show that's relevant to that expertise.

For example, if I had a podcast that was all about tech and software, I probably wouldn't invite a fitness coach as a guest to talk about their fitness strategies. I might be better served by inviting a company that has built software for fitness coaches to help them improve their coaching strategies. Or if I had a podcast that was all about marketing and sales, I probably wouldn't invite nurses and teachers as guests, as it's not relevant to their field of expertise. If I had a podcast that dealt with health and wellness, I would identify every health and wellness professional company and category that would be a relevant addition to my podcast and rank them based on which would be the most valuable additions to my network. Then I would make those invites.

So, choose a niche and a theme, create a simple cover and podcast name that would be relevant and compelling to that niche and theme, and then choose content that would also be relevant and compelling to that theme. You can use tools like Riverside or Zoom to record your podcasts. You can use tools like Descript to edit and transcribe the podcast, and use others to edit the video and create reels that you can give as gifts to your guests. I would start by trying to release one episode per week to stay consistent and then scale up from there as you find success.

The Reverse Guesting Strategy—How to Get on Top Podcasts (Even Without an Audience)

The "reverse guesting game plan" is how you can leverage other people's platforms and podcasts to get more viewership and perceived authority while building or running your podcast. The goal here is to identify the right types of shows that you would be a good fit for, so don't aim for *The Joe Rogan Experience* to start, as that would be nearly impossible to get on.

You need to identify the industries and podcast types that would be looking for content like yours. You can use tools like Listen Notes, PodMatch,

Rephonic, or even Apple's related shows feature to find some of the top podcasts that have anywhere from five hundred to five thousand listeners that would be a great fit to start your guesting journey on.

To do this, you're going to want to craft an irresistible hook. You're pitching your story and why that would make a compelling episode, but also, they're going to be looking at your social status. If they can't find you online, or what they find doesn't communicate that you are an expert, then you're not likely to get the guest spots.

This is where writing your book first is usually a great idea. The book gives you instant authority and icon status in your industry while simultaneously giving you amazing and very structured content that you can use on your podcast as well as on other people's podcasts as a guest. One of the things we'll talk about in the future chapter is using your book to create your signature speech, and there can be different variations of this. There can be a 30- to 60-second elevator pitch variation, up to an hour-long podcast variation, and everything in between.

Once you've crafted a compelling hook or story, you're going to want to reach out to these podcast hosts via email or some of the previously listed platforms and let them know that you love their show. Feed their ego and let them know that you think you'd be an ideal guest because…and then insert your two- to three-sentence hook here about why you would be an addition to their show.

It's also worth it to provide three to five unique topics or episode titles that you know will resonate with them to make it easy for them. If you've done past podcast interviews that have gone well, then you can send them some examples and links to those so they can see how you did. The more podcast episodes you do on your show and the more guest appearances you have, the easier it will get.

As you continue to build your authority and social status online, it will just continue to get easier and easier for you. I would aim for one guest spot per week on a new podcast, which would give you fifty-two opportunities throughout the year to position yourself as the expert in your industry, and I would ask the host for the raw and edited podcast content so you can use it in your marketing online.

Ensure that in every podcast you go into as a guest, you know the host's name, their journey, and what they like to talk about. Make sure to give your best performance, and don't go into it by the seat of your pants. Be prepared to give away your best stuff for free with a powerful call to action at the end that invites guests to go deeper with you after the show.

Now, beforehand, make sure that the host is okay with you doing that, and if they are, make sure that you provide them with motivating incentives for every sale that might happen. They're more likely to invite you back if there's a good experience. Once you have the content, you can turn it into tweets, reels, carousels, blog posts, emails, YouTube videos, and more to continue increasing your online visibility.

If somebody were to google your name six months from now, would they find that you are an author, that you are a podcast host, that you have tons of content and articles written, and would they see lots of YouTube links to podcast interviews that you've done on a range of topics? That is what you're going for. You want to leverage the halo effect by guesting on other people's podcasts. Remember, the halo effect says that if people perceive you to be an expert in one area, they are more likely to think that you are an expert in others as well.

The more podcasts you get to be a guest on, the more experience, content, backlinks, and exposure you get. This means that you will continue to get better and better podcast guest opportunities. It's also a great way to make new business friends if one of the podcasters on whose show you were a guest would also be a great guest on yours. On the back end, you can add them to your network as a business connection, friend, and, eventually, as a referral or strategic partnership.

Starting a podcast is about more than recording conversations; it's about opening doors. When you position yourself as the host, you create opportunities to connect with the very people who can elevate your brand, expand your network, and help you reach icon status. The guest strategy is your way of borrowing credibility today while building lasting authority for tomorrow.

CHAPTER 5

The Stage—How Speaking Makes You Unforgettable

Why Public Speaking is the Fastest Credibility Booster

Public speaking is one of the fastest ways to build credibility because it positions you as an authority. It also builds trust instantly, and it provides you with amazing social proof all at once. There are **six different ways** public speaking boosts your authority and impact:

1. **Instant authority and expertise:** When you're on stage—or even on a podcast or webinar—people immediately perceive you as an expert. The act of speaking publicly conveys credibility before you say a word. Unlike written content, live audiences are more inclined to listen and accept your authority, giving you instant thought leadership status.

2. **Trust and rapport at scale:** Speaking allows people to experience your personality, confidence, and knowledge in real time. Your tone, body language, and delivery help create a genuine connection—building trust far faster than articles or social media posts ever could.

3. **Social proof and perceived influence:** Sharing a stage with well-known thought leaders, like Russell Brunson or Tony Robbins, instantly elevates your perceived authority. Being invited to speak by an event, podcast, or organization also acts as a third-party endorsement of your credibility.

4. **Leverage and visibility:** Speaking puts you in front of dozens, hundreds, or even thousands of people at once. Recordings of your talks can be repurposed for long-term reach via platforms like YouTube, social media, and email newsletters—extending your influence well beyond the live moment.

5. **Leads and opportunities:** A powerful presentation often results in new business: clients, partnerships, podcast invites, or speaking gigs. People remember speakers—and they refer them. Speaking can become a magnet for high-quality connections.

6. **Positioning over competition:** While many people produce online content, few step up to speak in public. This instantly differentiates you from your competition, positioning you as someone who leads from the front rather than staying behind the scenes.

Important: If you want to establish credibility in your industry quickly, then speaking is one of the highest-impact activities you can engage in and leverage.

Here are three powerful examples of people who used public speaking to rapidly boost their credibility and authority in their respective industries:

1. Tony Robbins—Personal Development & Business Coaching

- Tony Robbins started as a seminar promoter for Jim Rohn before transitioning into his own speaking career.

- Through public speaking, he quickly established himself as an authority in personal development.

- His high-energy live events, TED talks, and interviews helped him gain credibility, leading to best-selling books, coaching clients, and corporate consulting deals.

- His massive impact today stems largely from his ability to connect with audiences through speaking.

2. Gary Vaynerchuk—Marketing & Entrepreneurship

- Gary Vee leveraged public speaking to transition from running a family liquor store to becoming one of the biggest names in digital marketing.

- He first gained traction by speaking at tech and marketing conferences, where he showcased his expertise in social media and brand building.

- His no-BS speaking style helped him gain credibility, which led to business opportunities, book deals, and the growth of VaynerMedia.

3. Brené Brown—Researcher & Author (Vulnerability & Leadership)

- Brené Brown was a relatively unknown researcher until her TED talk "The Power of Vulnerability" went viral.

- That one speech skyrocketed her credibility, leading to book deals, media appearances, and consulting work with Fortune 500 companies.

- Public speaking turned her from an academic into a mainstream thought leader.

Each of these people leveraged speaking engagements, conferences, and viral talks to boost their authority in record time. Do you want to explore a strategy for using public speaking in your business?

CHAPTER 6

Hosting Industry Awards & Recognitions

The Power of Being the One Who Recognizes Others

When you're the one recognizing other people, it completely changes the game. You're not chasing attention or trying to convince anyone you're legit; you're just showing up and saying, "I see greatness in this person, and I want to acknowledge it."

When you do that, people naturally assume that you've got the authority to make that kind of call. It's not loud or flashy. People just start looking at you as the one who spots talent: the connector, the curator. You're not competing for space anymore; you're defining it, and that shift in perception matters. It's what gets people to pay attention.

And here's the thing: people crave recognition, especially high performers. They might act like they don't, but everyone wants to be seen, especially by someone they respect, so when you're the one giving that out, when you're lifting others up, it makes you magnetic. People want to be around someone who recognizes value in others. It makes them feel important, and it makes them trust you.

That's where the psychological side kicks in, gratitude, reciprocity, all that good stuff. They remember who gave them the spotlight. They'll repost you, shout you out, and send people your way. It builds real relationships, not just followers or likes.

I'm not talking about needing to be some big media outlet, either. You don't need a massive platform. Just look at things like *Forbes'* 30 under 30 or *Inc.* 5000; those things change careers. The same is true with smaller stuff like "Top Ten Coaches in Austin" or "Best Founders Under 40." People love that stuff. It gives them a badge of honor, and they share it like crazy.

Meanwhile, the person who created the list is instantly seen as someone who's plugged in, someone with taste, someone who matters. That can be you. Even if you're just starting out, you can create something meaningful that puts other people on the map, and while you're doing that, you're quietly putting yourself on the map, too.

If you're trying to build authority without shouting about yourself all the time, this is the way to do it. Recognize others. Be the one who spots the greats. That alone sets you apart.

How to Launch an Industry Award (Even Without a Big Audience)

How do you launch an industry award when you don't have a big audience? Honestly, it's far more doable than people think. You don't need a massive following or some verified checkmark next to your name. What you need is clarity, intention, and a little bit of structure.

Start by picking a niche, and the more specific, the better. Don't just do "Top Entrepreneurs." Do "Top Ten Wellness Coaches in LA" or "Most Innovative

50

Sales Leaders Under 40." Make it feel like it's for a very particular group of people who would actually care about being featured.

Once you've got your angle, give it a solid name, something simple but polished. Add the year to make it feel like a tradition. People love stuff like "2025 Founders to Watch" or the "Bold Leader Awards." It doesn't have to be fancy, just clear and credible. Then set up a basic nomination form. You don't need a custom site or anything wild; just collect names, links, maybe a short description of what they do, and boom, you're in business.

Now, here's the trick: make it look like a big deal, even if it's your first time. Create a clean landing page. Use Canva or hire someone from Fiverr to design a logo and a digital badge, something people can post once they're selected. The badge is key. It gives winners something visual to share, and when they do, they're promoting you and your brand without even realizing it.

When it's time to announce the winners, tag them. Write a little caption about why they stood out. Keep it warm and real. You don't need a red carpet or a physical trophy. Most people are just honored to be recognized, and even if it's only five or ten winners, make it feel important. Treat it with respect, and other people will, too.

Here's the cool part. You can use the whole thing as content. Share the nominations, post the results, interview a couple of the winners, and turn it into a short email series or podcast episode. One little award turns into weeks of engagement, and if you do it right, the second time you run it, people will ask to be included. You'll get tagged. You'll get DMs. People will see you as the one who shines the light, and that light, even if it starts small, gets brighter quickly.

Don't overthink it. You don't need to wait until you're big enough. You just need to start with the audience you have and build something that makes other people feel seen. That's how movements start.

Leveraging Awards for Media, Networking, and Positioning Yourself as an Authority

Here's how you actually start leveraging these awards once you've got them. This is where things really start to move because the award is just the first domino. When used correctly, it becomes a tool for media exposure, networking, and positioning yourself as an authority—without coming across as "look at me."

Let's start with the media. The media loves recognition stories, especially if they're community-based or industry-specific, like "local business owner launches awards for emerging female founders." That's the kind of thing small press eats up, even bigger outlets if it's framed right. So, write a little press release, pitch it to some blogs or local media newsletters. Even if only one picks it up, it's still instant credibility, and you can use that in your content, like "as seen in" or "featured on." That starts building your perceived authority without you having to hype yourself up.

Now comes networking. This is the magic part because you now have a reason to reach out to literally anyone you want. Let's say there's someone you've been wanting to connect with for a while, but you haven't had a warm way in. Now you do: "Hey, I'm running a recognition series for the most innovative people in your space, and you were nominated," or "I'd love to feature you."

Boom. That changes the dynamic. You're not asking for anything; you're offering them something. When people feel seen and valued, they remember you, they follow you, they share you, and that opens the door for future conversations, partnerships, referrals, all of it.

Finally, there's positioning. This is the longer-term play. Every time someone shares their award, badge tags you in a post, or mentions you in a story, you're getting organic visibility, and every single one of those touchpoints builds your brand. You're quietly establishing yourself as the go-to person in the space, not because you said so but because others keep confirming it. The more consistently you show up in that curator role, the more people associate your name with quality, leadership, and connection. That's what shifts your brand from invisible to respected.

The award is the first move, but what you do after that creates the real impact. Don't just let it be a one-time thing. Turn it into a wave of content, connection, and credibility that keeps building long after the winners are announced.

CHAPTER 7

Leveraging a Signature Event or Conference

A signature event is a unique, often recurring event that builds brand authority, attracts your ideal audience, and creates a high-value environment for networking and sales. There are a few different ways that you can leverage them. By building authority, you position yourself as the go-to expert in your industry, generating leads and sales.

The next way to leverage a signature event is by creating an ecosystem. These events help you bring together the community you have created. Obviously, you're growing your community even bigger with each signature event that you do, but they also bring partners and influencers together in one room.

Signature events also increase brand loyalty. A well-run event makes attendees feel as if they're part of a movement, strengthening long-term relationships. Russell Brunson, whom we discussed in previous chapters, draws massive audiences for his events, and the dopamine hits that attendees get lead to him getting more sales. Or look at SaaS companies. Every year, they hold a massive event with a minimum of ten thousand people attending, where different companies and agencies white label their products or resell them in some way, shape, or form. By doing this, they keep their products top of mind.

The last way to leverage such events is that they can be used to attract media and partnerships. High-quality events can grab the press' attention and strategic collaboration. For example, if you post videos from the event on YouTube, Instagram, or LinkedIn, there's a strong chance people will see them and reach out to you—for collaborations, article features, or even invitations to future events.

Why Owning an Event Beats Just Speaking at Them

Speaking at any event is great for exposure, but owning the event gives you full control and long-term leverage. There are a number of reasons for this:

1. **You control the audience**
   You decide who attends and how they interact with your brand. This is your opportunity to bring in your ideal customer profile (ICP).
   If you're part of another event or networking community, it's not your network or ICP—it's more like a wild jungle. Hosting your own event is like cultivating your own farm.

2. **You own the revenue**
   Instead of just earning a speaker's fee—or speaking for free—you can monetize through ticket sales, sponsorships, upsells, and backend offers.

3. **You set the narrative**
   As the host, you control the agenda and messaging. You can align the entire experience with your business goals and guide attendees down a strategic customer journey.

4. **You build the community**

   Attendees associate the event with your brand, fostering long-term loyalty. Those who attend will remember the experience; those who miss it will want to be at the next one.

5. **You create recurring revenue**

   A successful event can be replicated annually or even more often. It can evolve into a membership or ongoing community platform.

The "Funnel Hacking Live" Effect—How Top Entrepreneurs Use Events to Control the Market

Russell Brunson's Funnel Hacking Live (FHL) is a master class on how events can dominate an industry. Here are a couple of ways that he does it. The first is treating the event as a sales funnel. FHL attracts entrepreneurs, educates them, and seamlessly moves them into high-ticket click funnel programs.

The second is something called "tribal branding." This is where the event creates a movement, making attendees feel like they're a part of an elite community.

The next point is strategic content flow. Every speaker, panel, and session leads into an offer, guiding attendees toward buying.

Next is high-energy, high-ticket conversions. The environment is designed to create urgency and excitement, leading to massive sales at the event. One of our partners, Justin, used to belong to a direct-selling company called Vemma, which was essentially a movement to help kids eat healthier and, more importantly, drink healthier energy drinks. This was the first-ever energy drink designed with mangosteen and all healthy vitamins. The idea was to go into your network, find people who wanted to be a part of a closed-door event, something at your home, at a restaurant, wherever, where you could speak about the movement and get everybody hyped up with very quick dopamine hits so that they essentially gave you their credit card right away and joined the movement.

The last point is exclusive announcements. This is where you're launching. Are you going to be doing product launches or special offers to make attendees feel like insiders? The goal is that once they are a part of your network, once they are "drinking your Kool-Aid," you're going to continuously give them dopamine hits by offering free downloadable PDFs, books that you wrote, product and service launches—things like that.

As you can see, Russell Brunson doesn't just host an event; he engineers a high-converting, high-retention experience that keeps people coming back year after year.

Step by Step—Hosting a Profitable Virtual or In-Person Event

The last piece of this puzzle is hosting a profitable virtual or in-person event. This should happen in eight different steps.

- **Step 1** is defining your goal and audience. Who is the event for, and what do you want them to do afterward? For example, are they going to buy a high-ticket offer, join a mastermind, etc.? So, discover who your ICP is, figure out their pain point, and then host an event of some sort that is going to cater to that person and solve that pain point.

- **Step 2** is choosing your format. Is this event going to be virtual, an in-person hybrid, a live event, a workshop, or a summit? This is very important to your ICP. If you're dealing with local people, obviously, you want some sort of local event. You don't want something that's halfway across the world. If you're a global digital advertising agency, then you might have to look more at virtual events.

- **Step 3** is crafting an irresistible offer. Give people a strong reason to attend, VIP perks, things that they can only get if they show up. This can be anything where they feel like the takeaway is not just educational, but tangible, perhaps even something that they can hold in their hands.

- **Step 4** is building the funnel. Create a compelling landing page. Create email sequences to drive registration. This isn't just for the top of the funnel but for everything that happens afterward. You can reach out to people who are already in your network, like if you have a strong LinkedIn profile, but you can also do this cold if you're doing Facebook ads. Either way, you want to drive them to a landing page that shows you off as the ultimate authority.

Let them know why they should attend your event. It has to be an irresistible offer combined with the authority to say, "This is something that you can't miss." You want them to experience the "fear of missing out" effect. You also want to capture their data and nurture them using email sequences after they register, so that you can ensure you stay top of mind.

- **Step 5** is monetization, so charge for tickets, offer sponsorships, upsell courses, or launch a product at the event. An irresistible offer can be something that you launch specifically for the event attendees. For example, it could be a new service or a very exclusive promotion, something that nobody can get outside the event.

- **Step 6** is creating an engaging experience. Even though you are the owner of the event, you still want to have other speakers. You don't want the event to be all about you; that can get pretty boring and stale very quickly. Instead, you want to bring on dynamic speakers, people who are industry leaders, authorities, and icons. You want to have interactive workshops, speaking sessions, and high-value takeaways.

- **Step 7** is to capture and convert; get attendees' contact info. Offer bonuses for action-takers, and follow up after the event with some sort of sales sequence.

- **Step 8** is building continuity. Turn event attendees into long-term customers through memberships, masterminds, and annual events. Once you've captured them, if done properly, there should be no reason why you can't capture them again and again and keep them coming back for more. Again, you want them to keep drinking that "Kool-Aid."

CHAPTER 8

Digital Communities—Why You Must Build (Not Just Join) Networks

There are three reasons why you should not just join a network but build one.

First, it allows you to control the conversation, so instead of adapting to someone else's rules, you shape the discussions and themes to align with your business goals. When you are the creator, you get to control every aspect of the game.

Second, you become the connector. Naturally, people look up to the person who brings others together, so by making yourself the connector, you position yourself as the industry authority.

Third, you own the relationships. This means that when you build a community, people trust you as their main source of information, opportunities, and business connections.

Why Owning a Mastermind, Networking Group, or Digital Community Makes You an Industry Leader

Being the creator of a networking group, mastermind, or online community puts you in an elite category. First, as you're building your authority, you're no longer just someone in the industry. You've become the go-to person for insights, partnerships, and opportunities. When someone can look you up online and see that you have this community, it automatically makes them think that you know what you're talking about.

Most people who are quiet in the industry are either new business owners trying to hustle or those who are really bad at social media and networking; either way, that doesn't leave them in a good position. A well-run group attracts qualified prospects who already trust you before you even pitch an offer, especially if you're giving them free knowledge and education.

If you offer a free course that people instantly get value from and they know that it came from you, they've unknowingly already become potential customers because they've bought into what you're saying. The best part is that if you own this group or network, members look up to you for leadership insights and recommendations, making it easier to guide them toward your solutions. What you'll see is that your Instagram account will get more followers, your LinkedIn account will get more connections, and everything will start to grow simultaneously because people are just interested in drinking your "Kool-Aid."

How to Create High-Value Digital Communities That People Want to Be Part Of

Let's talk for a second about how to actually create a high-value digital community or network that people want to be a part of. I still remember the early days when I had a community of sixteen people. The weight on my shoulders seemed immense, and I felt that my friends and family were laughing at me because I hadn't made it. It makes me laugh now because you can have a very successful business, but the moment you start a community and put yourself out there on social media, it's like you're starting back at zero and own nothing.

Eventually, I gave up that weight and realized that this was what everybody went through. Most people who have already made it have a huge community and following, and they never talk about the early days, when they had only a hundred followers and no likes every time they posted, despite posting multiple times a day.

It's a journey of discovery. You need to figure out your niche, define what you want to talk about, understand who you are, and clarify what you're truly building this audience for and what that means. The reality is, most people give up. I've seen countless individuals start building communities or social media profiles, posting consistently and offering value through courses, free PDFs, downloads, and LinkedIn groups. But over time, they abandoned it all because they felt it wasn't growing fast enough.

What people don't realize is that your first followers are not just your audience; they're your first customers and your early adopters. The companies that survive in 2025 won't be separated by the quality of their product alone, but by the value that they bring to their audience or community, and whether that community cares about what you have to say.

So, let's talk about how you can actually **create a high-value community** that people want to join:

1. **Define the core mission.** What problem does your community solve? Who is it for? What makes it different from existing groups?

2. **Choose the right platform**, such as Facebook groups, Discord school communities, Slack, or a private membership site.

3. **Make it exclusive.** Require applications, charge a fee, or set a clear membership standard to increase perceived value.

4. **Provide premium content.** Host live Q&As. Share insider knowledge and facilitate high-level discussions that members can't get elsewhere.

5. **Foster engagement.** Encourage networking, collaborations, and discussions that make members feel like they must be involved.

6. **Introduce monetization.** Offer premium memberships, paid mastermind sponsorships, or high-ticket consulting for members who want the next level of access.

7. **Scale with systems.** Use automation, content schedules, and community managers to keep engagement high without consuming all your time.

CHAPTER 9

Becoming a High-Level Connector

The fastest way to level up your influence opportunities and status isn't through content, ads, or even your skills. It's through who you know and, more importantly, who knows you. High-level connectors aren't just networkers; they're gatekeepers of opportunity, the people who facilitate deals, make introductions, and create rooms where things happen. If you can become that person, the one who brings the right people together, you'll never have to chase opportunities because they'll come to you. If you master this, you'll never have to sell yourself again because the right people will already be talking to you.

The Shortcut to Icon Status—Who You Know

You've probably heard the saying many times: "Your network is your net worth." However, when we say it, we don't mean it in the cliché, handshake-at-a-networking-event kind of way. Rather, it's referring to the person who can text three industry players and get deals moving in a day, who gets invited into rooms most people don't even know exist, and whom everyone thinks of when they say, "You know who you should talk to?" That's what high-level connectors do, and if you're not already one, here's how to become one from scratch.

The Rolodex Strategy—How to Build a High-Value Network From Scratch

You don't need fame, money, or status to build a powerful network. You just need intention and follow-through. Here's how the "Rolodex strategy" works:

1. **Identify 25:** Make a list of 25 people in your industry—or adjacent industries—who are doing interesting things. Focus on people you genuinely like, want to learn from, or collaborate with. This isn't about pitching; it's about building relationships.

2. **Give first:** Don't start with what you need—start with value. Introduce them to someone helpful, send a useful resource, or promote something they've created without expecting anything in return. This builds trust and sets up the law of reciprocity.

3. **Stay warm:** Use a simple CRM or even a Notes app to track follow-ups. Check in every 30 to 60 days. Congratulate them on launches, awards, or standout posts. Stay present and top of mind, without being pushy.

4. **Become the connector:** When someone needs a developer, designer, speaker, or partner—connect them. Even if it doesn't benefit you directly, you're building social capital. This is how strangers become contacts, contacts become collaborators, and collaborators become lifelong allies.

How to Host Invite-Only Dinners, Mastermind Sessions, and Vip Networking Events

The real power move is becoming the host of the room, so once you have a small but solid network, shift into host mode. People remember the person who brought everyone together. It's one of the fastest ways to establish yourself as a leader without having to say a word.

So, let's talk about how to host invite-only dinners, masterminds, and VIP events.

1. **Start small:** Four to eight hand-picked people are enough. Focus on quality over quantity.

2. **Curate the room:** Invite people who are interesting, not just important. Think creators, operators, founders, and investors—those who will vibe, not just network.

3. **Pick a format:** Choose a structure that fits your goal: private dinner, virtual mastermind, weekend retreat, coworking session, or brunch. Keep it intentional and structured to foster real connection.

4. **Make it feel exclusive:** Give it a name. Create a theme. People want to be part of something that has a "why" and a clear identity.

5. **Don't sell—facilitate:** Your role isn't to pitch. It's to orchestrate the experience. Let others shine, create meaningful connections, and be the glue that holds it together.

6. **Follow up:** Send thank-you messages, make post-event introductions, and keep the group active through platforms like Telegram, WhatsApp, or other community tools.

Here's why this works. When you become the connector, three powerful things happen. One, trust accelerates. People trust those who introduce them to someone valuable. Two, opportunities multiply. Every relationship becomes a doorway to more. Three, status increases. You're not asking to be in the room; you're hosting it, and people talk about the host long after the party's over.

Imagine that one of your friends is hosting an event. You walk into their house for an evening dinner, and candles are everywhere, the lights are beautifully dimmed, there's music in the background, and there are drinks, laughter, and good food. Such an experience will leave its mark, and you will remember that event and the friend who hosted it.

In a world chasing attention, be the person who builds connections. Becoming a high-level connector isn't just a career move; it's a legacy play. It cements your icon status. It's how you build movements, ecosystems, and empires, and it all starts with one intentional connection.

CHAPTER 10

Building an Industry Certification or Training Program

Why certifying others makes YOU the authority

Here's something that clicked for me when I started thinking about building a certification: it's that moment where you stop being just the person who *does* the thing and become the person who *teaches* it. You go from being the expert to being the educator. That's a big leap in positioning because now you're not just saying, "Hey, I'm good at this," you're saying, "I've built something good enough that others can learn it, use it, and succeed with it."

That shift turns you into an authority, not because you said so, but because other people start representing your work out in the world. That's where the real trust kicks in. People look at you differently when you're the one who trains the pros. They think, "Oh, you're not just the expert. You're the one who *creates* experts." It's authority by endorsement, and that holds more weight than any resume or testimonial because it means someone else is carrying your method and putting their name behind it, and they're proud to do it.

That's powerful, and it turns into social proof at scale. You certify ten people, twenty, fifty, and now you've got all these walking, breathing testimonials out there talking about your work, using your frameworks, getting results, and tagging you in their stuff, and every single one of them becomes part of this bigger ecosystem you're building. It's not just marketing; it's identity. They're part of something, and that creates loyalty that lasts much longer than just a course.

What you're really doing is giving people a stamp of approval, and we all know how much that matters in today's world. People want that credibility, that badge that says, "Yeah, I trained under this person, and I know what I'm doing." If your framework is solid and the content is dialed in, that stamp becomes the standard in your niche.

That's how industries are shaped. Someone just decides that this is the method, and then they build it into a system and certify others to use it. Suddenly, that method becomes the benchmark. The cool part is that it levels up your personal brand, too, because now you've got your own framework, your own language, your own way of doing things, and it becomes part of your identity.

It's not just what you know; it's what you *teach*. That forces you to get really clear on your IP: What's actually working? What are the steps? What are the outcomes? How do you make it teachable and repeatable? All of that just sharpens your positioning in the market, and honestly, there's this whole psychological aspect, too. We naturally respect teachers, mentors, and coaches, the people who pass things down. It's built into how we see leadership. We don't just admire talent; we admire the people who share it and multiply it.

So, yeah, certifying others, that's how you stop being the player and become the playbook.

How Industry Leaders Create Certifications That Build Loyalty and Credibility

Here's how the real leaders are building certifications that actually stick and create real long-term loyalty. It all starts with designing the thing in a way that actually delivers results. It's not about dumping a bunch of info into a course platform and calling it a certification. It's about reverse-engineering the outcome you want people to have and building the program backward from that. You start by asking, "What does someone need to *do* or *achieve* in the real world for this to feel legit?" and then you shape everything around that outcome.

The best ones also create a sense of community, not just "Hey, go through the content at your own pace," but "You're now part of something." You've got this shared identity with others who've been through the same system, with the same standards and the same language. When you build that inner circle, it becomes a real brand asset. People start introducing themselves, like, "Hey, I'm a certified [XYZ] coach, strategist, or whatever," and that becomes a part of how they see themselves.

Structure matters more than people think. The way you break it down into modules or levels adds perceived value. It makes it feel professional, organized, and easier to complete. Don't just throw a bunch of lessons in a folder. Instead, actually map out the transformation step by step and build in things like practice assignments, real-world applications, milestones, and check-ins. That kind of stuff makes it feel more like a real credential than just another info product.

Now let's talk about language because this is something I see a lot. A course and a certification program might have the same content, but they feel completely different. "Certification" says mastery. It says completion. It says endorsement, and people will literally pay more just because of how it's framed. So, don't undersell it.

This is a status thing, too, and that's not bad. Humans are wired to chase that stuff, and support is huge. The difference between a course someone never finishes and a certification someone *proudly* completes is often just a little bit of accountability, some coaching, and maybe a group call or a check-in message. When people feel supported, they're much more likely to finish and tell others about it, and that's where the loyalty kicks in, because they don't just remember the content; they remember how they felt going through it.

And don't sleep on badges. We're living in a credential economy. People love digital proof that they can put on LinkedIn, websites, email signatures, social profiles, or whatever. Give them something they can show off, and they will. When they do, they're promoting your brand without you asking.

Then there's the alumni angle. Once someone's certified, keep them in the ecosystem. Feature their wins. Refer clients to them. Pull them into partner opportunities. The certification doesn't have to be the end of the relationship; it can be the beginning of a whole network, and that's when referrals and credibility start compounding.

The $10M Certification Model—How to Create a Profitable Expert Program

This is where it all comes together. This is how you take what you know and turn it into a real business asset, a legit revenue stream that can scale without burning you out. It starts with your method, your framework, whatever it is you do that works. You turn that into something teachable and repeatable, a system people can follow and get results from. That becomes your flagship offer, the foundation of your certification.

When it comes to the way you deliver it, you've got a few options. Honestly, it depends on your style and your audience. Some people love doing live cohorts, where everyone goes through it together. Some prefer evergreen so that people can start anytime. Some do hybrid, which is kind of the best of both. It's less about choosing the perfect model and more about choosing what you'll actually stick with and what gets people through to the finish line.

Then there's pricing. This is where people often overthink things, but here's the deal: if you're certifying someone, you're not just giving them content; you're giving them a license to use your method, and that's valuable. So, you can charge a one-time fee, sure, but you can also do licensing or even a subscription, where they pay for continued access or updated materials. That recurring piece can be a game-changer.

Once you've got your first few people through it, you've got the potential to scale. Maybe one of your certified folks becomes a trainer. Maybe you bring on affiliates or licensing partners who teach your method under your brand. Now you're multiplying reach without doing all the delivery yourself, and that's how it starts to grow beyond you.

I'm not going to get deep into the tech, but you'll need something to host your content and maybe some automation to make things run smoothly—but honestly, keep it simple. When you're starting out, the most important thing is making sure the experience is clean and people are actually learning and implementing. One of the best platforms out there for this kind of thing is Skool. It's super clean and easy to use, and it gives you that community feel without needing to overcomplicate anything.

Marketing is all about positioning and proof, and you build social proof with your early students. Get some testimonials. Create a little buzz. Maybe use a waitlist or limit enrollment to create a bit of scarcity. That makes people pay attention and want to be part of it. Over time, what really compounds your marketing is your success stories, when your certified people are out there crushing it and telling the world where they learned it from. That's your best marketing, and every new cohort adds more fuel to the fire.

Eventually, this thing can become a whole ecosystem. Your certification can feed into retreats, masterminds, software, and group coaching. It becomes a hub that everything else connects to, and a platform like Skool makes it easy to build that kind of sticky container where your people stay plugged in and engaged. That's when it really starts to feel like a business that runs deeper than just selling info. Now it's a brand, a movement, a methodology that lives beyond you.

CHAPTER 11

The YouTube & Media Authority Strategy

Attention is the new currency, and trust is the compound interest. If you want to be seen as the go-to expert in your niche, owning media is no longer optional. Whether it's a YouTube channel, podcast, or LinkedIn video series, building your platform gives you the ultimate leverage.

First, you control the narrative. Second, you borrow credibility from high-status guests. Third, you position yourself as a thought leader without having to prove it. This strategy isn't about going viral; it's about creating evergreen authority content that builds long-term trust, generates inbound leads, and opens doors that cold DMs never will.

Let's break it down.

Why Owning a Media Platform Builds Massive Long-Term Trust

Here's why owning a media platform builds massive long-term trust. First, you're seen as the expert, not just because of what you say but because of the stage you've built. You're also always top of mind. Consistent, high-value content creates familiarity, and familiarity builds trust. People come to you rather than chasing leads, and your platform becomes a magnet for inbound opportunities. It scales your presence so you can speak to thousands at once while still feeling personally authentic, allowing you to become the source people turn to, not just another voice in the crowd.

The Interview Strategy—How to Leverage High-Status Guests

Interviewing respected experts or influencers is one of the fastest ways to build credibility and grow your audience. Here's how to do it right.

Start with your current network. You'd be surprised by who will say yes to a well-crafted invite. Second, focus on them. Make your interviews about elevating your guests, not showing off your knowledge. Third, extract stories, not sound bites. Great interviews go deep. They ask meaningful questions that let your guests shine.

Fourth, borrow authority. When your audience sees you side by side with respected names, they automatically elevate you. Last, repurpose content everywhere. Cut the best clips into carousel reels, LinkedIn posts, and email teasers. This is the fastest path to earning trust by association.

The YouTube/LinkedIn Video Playbook—How to Create Content That Positions You as the Expert

Let's talk about how to create content that positions you as an expert on YouTube and LinkedIn, something we call our "playbook."

1. **Expert Breakdowns:** Dissect trends, strategies, or case studies in your industry.
    Show that you have depth of knowledge, not just opinions.

2. **Authority Interviews:** Build a series of interviews with industry leaders—this becomes your own personal media tour and positions you alongside respected voices.

3. **Personal Insight Stories:** Share stories from your own journey, but always connect them to practical lessons your audience can apply.

4. **Frameworks and How-Tos:** Walk people through your unique frameworks, systems, or processes. This is how you go from being seen as "helpful" to "hirable."

Pro tips: Keep videos tight and focused. Three to ten minutes is perfect for YouTube, and one to three minutes is best for LinkedIn. Use strong hooks and titles that speak to problems and aspirations. Add captions and clean editing to boost retention.

Calls to action are everything. At the end, invite people to subscribe to your newsletter, join your community, or take the next step. And if you're using YouTube, always, always have a captivating graphic thumbnail, something that is clickbait.

Owning a media platform is how you scale trust, attract opportunity, and submit your authority without ever having to shout it out. The world follows those who create the conversation, and when you own the mic, you own the momentum.

PART 3

HOW TO SCALE YOUR ICON STATUS INTO A MOVEMENT

CHAPTER 12

The Psychology of Movements— Why Identity Drives Influence

Why People Join Movements, Not Businesses

People are wired to want to belong to tribes. In 1979, psychologist Henry Tajfel developed the social identity theory, which says that people define themselves by the groups they belong to. For example, they might buy from brands that affirm their self-image and support their aspirational self.

Social identity theory taps into the psychology of belonging, status, purpose, and recognition. The more your brand helps people feel like they might be the hero in their own story, the more they'll wear it and promote it proudly. Identity equals loyalty. People don't just want to buy something; they want to belong to something.

According to Maslow's hierarchy of needs, belonging is as essential as safety. We don't follow logos; we follow leaders who are leading movements. We rally behind their missions because we can identify with them. After all, they're who we are or who we want to become. Businesses sell services and focus on transactions to get clients. A movement sells purpose and identity. It focuses on transformation. It spreads a system of beliefs to get loyal followers.

Your goal is to turn your business into a movement, your offer into a belief system. Eighty percent of customers buy from brands whose mission aligns with their values and who they consider themselves to be. Brands that create tribes and communities of like-minded followers outperform traditional marketing by more than five times, and their retention ratios are even higher because people don't leave movements like they leave businesses.

Harley-Davidson sells the feeling of brotherhood, freedom, and rebellion, not motorcycles. ClickFunnels sells the identity of becoming a funnel hacker. That comes with badges, yearly events, club awards, merch, and a sense of belonging to something bigger. They don't just sell the tool; they sell the identity along with it. Nike doesn't sell shoes; it sells the identity of being athletic, competitive, ambitious, and driven. When Michael Jordan joined the ranks of Nike and started selling shoes, the slogan "Be Like Mike" was what people bought, not the shoes themselves. The shoes were just the fee to get into the club.

When taking the steps to turn your business into a movement, follow the acronym **M.O.V.E.**

- **M** stands for mission over marketing, where what you believe in goes beyond what you sell.

- **O** stands for offering identity, not just products.
  - You need to give people something to identify with.
  - Do you consider yourself a funnel hacker? A growth-driven CEO? A Freedom Queen?
  - What do you want to get behind?

- **V** stands for visual symbols and rituals.
  - Movements need symbols, slogans, rituals, and swag to remind people what they are a part of.

- o People get tattoos because they are symbolic of something bigger.
- o Symbols communicate *big* ideas concisely.
- o Human beings have always used symbolism to communicate the most important things.
- o Creating swag that people can wear to show off the movement is ritualistically important as much as it is materially important.
- o Symbols are a powerful piece of human psychology and communicate important things without having to do so explicitly, and they are an incredibly powerful tool if you want to create any type of movement.

- E stands for elevating the tribe.
  - o Creating opportunities inside a movement for members to shine by celebrating their wins, highlighting their successes, and showcasing their commitment to the movement creates a sense of belonging to a valuable tribe.

The dark side of failing to create a movement is staying invisible and expendable. Constantly chasing new leads, struggling to get new clients, continuously being a number on a spreadsheet and interchangeable with your competitors, where the only thing you get to compete on is price instead of passion, and losing clients as soon as your transactional relationship with them ends, is a slow and painful way to do business. Movements, on the other hand, create lifetime clients, raving fans, referrals, and high-net-worth networks. People feel compelled to invite friends into movements they're proud to be a part of.

How to Create an Identity Brand That People Want to Be Part Of

The key trait of an identity brand is that it stands for something bigger than its products or services. It gives people a label to adopt and identify with, like funnel hacker, icon, freedom rider, growth-driven CEO, Freedom Queen, etc. It has rituals, symbols, and language only insiders understand. It makes people feel proud to wear, share, and represent the brand, and it offers transformation, not just transactions. When your brand becomes iconic, your audience wants to be a part of it.

When building your brand, avoid these three big mistakes.

1. **Don't build your brand around you—build it around them:** Focus on your audience's needs, identity, and transformation, not just your personal story or achievements.

2. **Don't use vague values:** Make your values specific, bold, and lived out in everything you do. Generic values don't inspire loyalty—real ones do.

3. **Don't try to be for everyone:** Identity requires exclusivity. A strong us-versus-them mentality helps people identify with your movement and become passionate advocates.

Now identify what the big outcome is for the people who are a part of your brand. What are they identifying with? What will they get by being a part of the tribe and movement? What would make them proud to say and wear? What would make them excited to attend and do? And what types of people do they want to be surrounded by? Identify who's in the tribe and then create the brand around them. Then begin to add elements like events, swag, training, special guests, celebrations and awards, certifications, and upward mobility.

People not only want to belong to a movement, but they also want to be able to be promoted to positions of leadership within that movement. This means that another incredibly important part of your movement is to create a hierarchy of leadership, and the way they can get to the top positions of leadership is through your products and services.

Your logo doesn't matter as much as the language you use. Your tagline doesn't matter as much as the tribe you create. Your product is not your brand; the group identity is your brand, and if you do this, you give them something worth belonging to.

People want to belong, and buying your products and services is just a way for them to show their loyalty, excitement, and commitment to the movement.

CHAPTER 13

The Power of Awards & Accolades

How to Win Prestigious Awards and Certifications That Add Credibility

Let's talk about how to actually win awards that mean something—not just the fluffy participation stuff, but the ones that add real credibility to your brand and open doors.

First, you've got to be intentional. Look around your industry and figure out what awards actually matter. Where do the top players in your space get recognized? What logos are showing up on people's websites or LinkedIn headers? Those are your targets. Don't waste time chasing stuff no one's ever heard of. Focus on the ones that signal real trust and positioning.

Once you've found a few, study the past winners seriously. Read the write-ups, watch the interviews, whatever you can find, and try to reverse-engineer what the judges are rewarding. Are they focused on revenue growth, innovation impact, or community results? Once you know that, you can shape your story to highlight the things they value.

Speaking of story, don't just say what you did. Give them actual numbers. Give them transformation. Give them the before and after. This is where a strong application stands out. Throw in visuals if it makes sense: graphs, screenshots, quotes. Make it feel real and tangible, not just a wall of fluff and buzzwords.

Client testimonials, case studies, and even media mentions can take your submission to the next level. They're like backup evidence, showing that other people are already validating your work. That way, the judges aren't just taking your word for it; they're seeing a pattern of credibility and results from different angles.

And here's a move most people don't think of: use award deadlines as a reason to reflect and capture your wins. So many of us forget to document the good stuff because we're always in go mode, but when you've got an award submission coming up, it's the perfect excuse to pause, pull some numbers, grab a few stories, and actually capture what you've built.

Also, don't wait for someone to nominate you. Yeah, that's nice when it happens, but in most cases, you can nominate yourself or have a team member or colleague do it. It's not weird; it's actually really normal in a lot of spaces. No one's gonna think less of you for showing up; they'll think more of you for stepping up.

Apply every year because, even if you don't win the first time, your name starts to get familiar, and that repetition can work in your favor. Eventually, someone on that panel is going to say, "I remember this person from last year. Let's take a closer look." *Boom!* Now you're on the radar.

Finally, stack the small ones. Get those niche, local, or industry-specific awards under your belt first. They're easier to win. They give you early momentum, and then you can use those wins as stepping stones when you go after the big national stuff. They build your case piece by piece.

Why "Seen in Media" Validation Multiplies Business Opportunities

This is one of those things that makes a much bigger difference than most people realize. Just being *seen* in the media, even if it's not some huge feature, can totally change how people view you. The reason for this is that the media gives you perceived authority. The second someone sees your name next to *Forbes, Entrepreneur,* or even just on a local podcast, their brain goes, "Okay, this person's legit. They're getting attention from real outlets, not just talking about themselves online."

Those logos and brand names are shortcuts for trust. We're all kind of trained to respond to them. We might not even read the full article, but just seeing that badge on your site or LinkedIn profile changes the vibe. It puts you in a different category instantly, and when you're trying to get clients, land partnerships, or even just connect with higher-level people, having that media backing makes the whole process smoother. They trust you because someone else has already "co-signed" you.

And here's the kicker: it doesn't even have to be about metrics. People think that they need to have this crazy revenue story or huge social following to get press, but what really lands are stories about purpose, impact, and a unique perspective. If you've got a mission or a belief that stands out, that kind of story gets shared far more than a dry data dump, and when it does get shared, it travels further because it feels human and relatable.

Once you've got one or two pieces out there, you can repurpose the hell out of them. Throw the logos on your sales deck banner, your email signature, and maybe even your funnel header. It becomes a layer of social proof that works for you behind the scenes. Every time someone checks you out, you don't have to say you're credible. The media's already done it for you.

You don't have to start big, either. Start local. Pitch a niche podcast, business journal, or blog in your industry. Those smaller placements are easier to get and still carry weight. They start stacking and give you momentum. Then, when you pitch a bigger outlet later, you can say, "Here's where I've already been featured." That opens doors far more quickly than cold pitching from scratch.

What it really comes down to is that the media gives you a third-party voice, and that changes the game. It's not just you saying you're great; it's someone else telling the world, "This person is worth listening to." That kind of credibility leads to more referrals, more visibility, and many more business opportunities. It just works.

How to Leverage Third-Party Credibility for Higher Closing Rates

Here's the play when it comes to actually using third-party credibility to close more deals. It's not just about having the awards or media features; it's about *how* you bring them into the conversation. Instead of the prospect thinking, "Why should I trust this person?" you're shifting that whole dynamic to "How soon can we get started?" energy. That happens when you build in those credibility markers ahead of time, such as on sales calls or even just in casual conversations.

You don't need to come in bragging, but drop those accolades in naturally. For example, if you've been featured somewhere or won something, just weave it into the story: "Yeah, we rolled out this strategy last year, and it actually ended up landing us a top-ten spot on that awards list" or "We were recently featured in *Entrepreneur* for how we built our referral system." whatever it is, just make it feel like part of your journey, not a flex.

If you've got a team, make sure they know how to talk about this stuff, too, because when your team starts using language like "as seen in" or "our award-winning framework," it adds weight to everything else they say, especially if it's a sales or support convo. It builds consistency and reinforces trust.

Visuals matter, too. Throw those logos on your landing pages, lead magnets, and checkout pages. Make sure they're placed where people are making buying decisions because that's where the risk shows up in their mind, and those little trust cues help reduce that friction. They think, *Okay, other people have vetted this already. It's not just some random person on the internet.*

That's the bigger idea: you're not just selling your product or service; you're selling the feeling of being part of something established and trusted. When someone's deciding whether to invest, they're looking at whether you're safe, whether you're proven, and when they see that others have already said yes to you through media or awards, it makes that decision much easier.

You can also build this into your nurture sequences. Drop a story or interview you were featured in, maybe a link to an award announcement, just little touches that keep reinforcing your credibility without being pushy. The more touchpoints they see, the more familiar you become before you even hop on the call.

And seriously, if someone googles you before a meeting, which they probably will, what shows up should match what you're saying in the pitch. The story you're telling them on Zoom should already be supported by what they're seeing on your site, in your content, and on page one of search results. If it is, then the sale is just about timing, not trust.

CHAPTER 14

Leveraging AI & Technology for Authority Scaling

Why AI Levels the Playing Field for Icon Status

Here's what's wild about where we're at right now with AI: it has completely leveled the playing field. You used to need a full team of designers, writers, editors, and social media managers to look like a legit authority in your space. Now, with the right tools, you can pull that off solo. It's not even about budget anymore; it's about knowing how to leverage what's already available, and honestly, most people aren't even scratching the surface.

AI tools are letting solopreneurs compete with full-blown agencies. You can put out content that looks and sounds like it came from a media team, even if it's just you behind a laptop, and that changes the game because now you don't need to wait until you can afford help to start showing up as a leader. You can start looking like a leader *right now*, and speed is the new flex.

What used to take a week or two to write, design, and post now takes a couple of hours or even less. You can map out a month of content in an afternoon using the right prompts or tools, and *boom!* you're everywhere, you're top of mind, and it's not draining you. That's a massive shift for anyone trying to build authority without burning out.

What I've noticed, too, is that the smartest creators aren't focused on editing, formatting, or any of the technical stuff anymore. Instead, they're focused on the message, on what they actually want to say, because they know the tools can handle the rest. The game has become less about doing it all yourself and more about saying the right thing and letting tech carry the weight, and that's where leverage comes in.

Authority today isn't about who works the hardest; it's about who works the smartest and who uses leverage to stay consistent, polished, and visible because that's what builds trust: showing up again and again, looking sharp, sounding clear, and staying in your lane. People notice that, and they start putting you in the category of someone who's operating on another level.

Here's the thing. Perception of scale is real. People assume you're bigger than you are if you look the part, and AI lets you look the part. Without hiring five people, you can schedule posts, create graphics, send emails, and edit videos, all with tools that are either free or super-low cost, and it all works behind the scenes while you focus on higher-level stuff.

So, yeah, this whole AI wave is not just a trend; it's a shift in power, and the people who learn how to ride it early are gonna be the ones who look like the top players, even if they're building from their kitchen table. It's not about how big your team is anymore; it's about how you show up, and the tools are right there, waiting to make that easier than it's ever been.

How AI-Driven Content Keeps You Omnipresent Without Burnout

The biggest difference for me when it comes to AI and content is not just that it saves time. It's that it lets you show up *everywhere* without actually being everywhere. That's the game when you're trying to build authority. People need to see you, hear you, and read you consistently, and that's hard to do manually unless you've got a full team or no life.

However, AI changes that. You can literally take one piece of content, a podcast, a video, even just a quick idea you voice out, and repurpose it into ten different formats: blog post, LinkedIn carousel, email, YouTube short, Instagram reel, tweet thread—all of it. You also don't have to create from scratch over and over again because the tools help you spin content out fast and clean.

Honestly, voice-to-text has been a game-changer. I'll just talk out an idea while I'm driving or walking, and AI will turn that into a full blog script, training, or even the foundation for a book. It still sounds like *me*, but cleaner, more organized, and much easier to publish without having to stare at a blank doc for hours.

You can even plan content out for months ahead using AI schedulers or strategy tools. It'll help you map out what, where, and when to post, and suddenly, your brand is showing up daily without you scrambling every morning to figure out what to say that day. That part alone takes so much mental load off.

Then you've got all the smaller tools that add up: AI caption generators, AI email writers, carousel builders. All that little repetitive stuff that usually drains your energy is now handled, and AI keeps your content sharp, fresh, and consistent without the stress.

When people see you showing up all the time, they start trusting you. They think, *Okay, this person's the real deal. They're on it.* The best part is that you can automate the entire top of your funnel. All the posts, shares, and initial brand touchpoints can be running in the background while you're focused on building relationships, serving clients, or creating your next offer. You're not stuck in content mode 24/7 anymore. AI basically clears the noise so your energy goes into the stuff that actually matters: the big vision, the strategy, and the people, not the tech.

Burnout happens when you're stuck doing all the tasks that don't move the needle, and AI gives you a way out. It lets you keep the visibility and momentum going while still protecting your bandwidth, and when you're building something long-term, that's everything.

The Future of Digital Branding—AI Avatars, Chatbots, and Automated Authority-Building

This is where things start getting really interesting. We're not just talking about using AI for content anymore. We're talking about building a digital version of yourself that works around the clock while you sleep, and the tools are already here for it.

You can create branded AI avatars that literally teach, coach, or consult for you 24/7. You train them on your content, voice, and frameworks, and suddenly, people are learning from you without you even being in the room.

The same thing is true with chatbots, but not those clunky robotic ones from five years ago. I'm talking about bots that actually sound like *you*, use your tone, understand your audience, and guide people through real conversations that build trust, answer questions, and even qualify leads. It's like having a mini-you handling the front end of your business in real time.

AI video tools are stepping it up, too. You can literally take one recording and turn it into a hundred variations with different hooks, intros, and lengths, with all of it handled for you, or even generate content from scratch based on your ideas without having to record anything yourself. That's scale on a whole new level.

Imagine someone landing on your website, and before they ever meet you, they're watching a video of your avatar explaining your method, walking them through your philosophy, maybe even giving them a next step based on what they need, and it still feels personal. It still feels like they're talking to you because the tech is that good now, and that changes everything. Your brand becomes a living, breathing system that runs 24/7, not just when you post something or go live. It's always on, always working, always building familiarity.

That's the future. You're not just a person anymore; you're a platform, and when people engage with your brand, they're engaging with this entire ecosystem that you've designed and trained to operate without you needing to show up every single day. Then you plug that into your funnel, nurture sequences, emails, and DM flows, and suddenly, you've got a whole customer journey built on automation that still feels human and warm but doesn't rely on your constant energy or time.

That's the shift. The next level of authority isn't about doing more; it's about building smarter systems that carry your presence forward consistently and strategically. This is where branding is headed. It's not just about having a good message; it's about designing an always-on version of you that educates, nurtures, and connects around the clock, and the people who start building that now are going to be light years ahead of everyone else.

CHAPTER 15

Automating & Scaling Your Icon Status

How to Keep Your Brand Top-of-Mind Without Doing All the Work

If you want to stay top of mind without constantly grinding, you've got to build what I call a "visibility engine," something that keeps running whether you're in launch mode, taking a break, or deep in delivery. Honestly, tools like GoHighLevel make this a thousand times easier. It's kind of like your whole content brain and back end in one place.

The first thing I do is map out content using a planning doc or voice notes. Then I drop that into GoHighLevel's social planner and schedule everything out thirty, sixty days in advance. Take a couple of hours, maybe once a month, to knock out the ideas, plug in the copy, add a few carousels or video clips, and *boom!* you've got a month of content dripping out across all your platforms without you thinking about it day to day.

You can also repurpose stuff straight from one place. Grab pieces of your podcast, blog, or even past emails and plug them into the system. Then use automation rules inside GoHighLevel to trigger different follow-ups or move leads through a funnel based on what people engage with. It's all running in the background while you do your actual work.

If you have a virtual or marketing assistant, you can delegate the whole process inside GoHighLevel. Let them repurpose, post, and respond to comments and update campaigns so that you're not stuck in the weeds doing the repetitive stuff. Your job is to create the vision, drop the raw ideas, and let the system distribute and follow up for you.

Then there's the email side. I've got evergreen welcome sequences built out in GoHighLevel that go out to every new lead. They introduce them to my world and tell them who I am, what I believe, and how I can help, all spaced out over a couple of weeks, and I don't touch it at all. Once it's set up, every new subscriber gets that same, consistent brand experience without me lifting a finger.

Batching is another big one. I'll set aside a day every few weeks to record some videos, write a few posts, and maybe even do a brain dump of voice notes. Then I plug everything into GoHighLevel to get chopped up, scheduled, and pushed out across email, social, and even SMS if we're doing a promo, all of it from one dashboard that's clean and super efficient.

Last, I set recurring blocks on my calendar to check in on all of it, maybe once a week, just to tweak, optimize, add a piece, or review what's working. That's it. No daily scrambling, no pressure, just clean brand momentum handled through automation. Honestly, when you've got a tool like GoHighLevel doing the heavy lifting, there's no excuse not to be visible. It's all right there; you just have to plug it in and let it run.

The Content Leverage Model—Reusing Books, Podcasts, and Stage Content to Flood the Internet

This is the part that most people sleep on. They do all this work to create something big, like a podcast, book, or keynote, and then they post about it once, maybe twice, and move on. The truth is that those things are gold mines if you know how to pull them apart. The content leverage model is all about squeezing every drop of value out of your long-form stuff and letting it work for you over and over again.

Let's say you've got a book chapter or a podcast episode, or you did a talk on stage. You can take that asset and break it down into ten, fifteen, even twenty smaller pieces. You can pull out quotes, frameworks, takeaways, behind-the-scenes clips, bloopers, whatever, and turn them into carousel reels, tweet threads, blog posts, or even just raw thoughts for email.

If you've done interviews or speaking gigs, grab those clips and turn them into Instagram reels or YouTube shorts. Just pull a 60-second soundbite, add subtitles, and throw it out there. That kind of stuff performs because it feels real and conversational, and it gives people a taste of your vibe without asking them to sit through a full hour.

If you're on someone else's podcast, don't just post the link once. That's solo content. Instead, break it down, take what you said, and repackage it as your own post, or turn your talking points into an email or carousel post. Suddenly, your audience is getting high-value content without you creating anything new from scratch.

This is where having a content vault comes in handy. I like to keep everything stored and sorted in one place. That way, I can just dip into the vault, pull something solid, and go. You can set this up in something simple, like Google Drive or Skool.

If you're running a community or content hub, load up that repurposed content, schedule it through the social planner, and drip it out through email newsletters or SMS campaigns, depending on the audience. Then just let it run. You've already done the hard part. Now the machine handles the follow-through.

You can even take your top-performing content and create a "greatest hits" series. Just recycle the stuff that people already loved because, honestly, most people didn't see it the first time, and if they did, they probably forgot. That repetition builds brand equity, and it makes you feel *everywhere* without being on a content treadmill. The idea is to be omnipresent through smart repackaging, not constant reinvention. Don't create from scratch.

The Partnership Play—How to Strategically Partner With Other Icons to Rise More Quickly

If you want to rise quickly and build real credibility, you don't do it alone; you find people who are already in motion and trusted by the kind of audience you want to serve, and you *build with them*. This isn't about clout chasing or pitching yourself all over the place; it's about aligning with people who complement what you do, not compete with it.

Start by looking for creators, thought leaders, and service providers who have a similar mission or vibe but offer something different from what you do. For example, if you do mindset coaching and they do branding, or you've got a tech platform and they do strategy, now you've got a crossover audience and value that doesn't overlap too much, and you can build something cool together.

Co-creating content is the easiest and most low-effort way to get started. Hop on a livestream together. Do a podcast swap or record a panel discussion that lives on both your channels. You're not just sharing content; you're sharing credibility because their audience now sees you as someone in their circle, and that trust transfers almost instantly.

If you've got an offer, platform, or certification, think about launching an affiliate or referral partnership, even just a simple setup where they get a percentage for every referral sent that leads to a sale. It creates a natural incentive to promote each other and grow together. You can do all of that inside something like GoHighLevel. Track referrals, set up automations, and follow up with leads. It's super clean.

Another move is joining or creating a mastermind, where this kind of thing is baked in. You get to know people and build trust over time, and the cross-promo happens naturally. You're not forcing anything; who you know becomes who you grow with, and that's where a lot of real leverage comes from.

You can even scale your method by offering powered-by or certified-by partnerships. Let others teach your framework under your brand or co-brand. It gives them credibility and you greater reach—a win-win that begins transforming your method into a movement. Then there's the more tactical stuff, like doing giveaways, bundles, micro-events, list shares, and visibility promos together. It doesn't have to be big to be effective. As you stack those small plays, they start to compound.

The biggest thing that I've learned is this: the more you act like a connector, the more valuable you become. Introduce people. Help them win. Make strategic intros that don't benefit you right away. People remember that. It builds social capital fast, and that currency goes far further than followers or likes.

So, if you want to rise quickly, don't do it alone. Link up with other icons and move together. The momentum hits much harder when you're building in good company.

CHAPTER 16

The Ultimate Test—What Happens When Someone Googles You?

Conducting Your Icon Audit—Are You Discoverable, Authoritative, and in Control of Your Narrative?

So, here's the real test of all this work. Forget what you say about yourself. Forget the pitch. Forget the profile. What happens when someone googles you? Seriously, open an incognito tab, type in your name, hit enter, and just sit with what shows up on page one. That's the version of you that most people are seeing before they ever talk to you, and it matters more than we like to admit.

So, is it intentional, or is it just a bunch of random stuff? Is it your old LinkedIn job from five years ago, a local article from something unrelated, or the brand you've been working to build, your current positioning, your authority, or your work? That's the question. If that's not showing up, then we've got some work to do.

Go through your social profiles, your website, any features or press links, and ask yourself, *Do these things actually reflect who I am right now and what I do, or are they just floating out there, disconnected from my current message?* If someone lands on your Instagram or LinkedIn page or your website and it feels like a different person or outdated, it breaks the trust before you even get started.

You also want to make sure that your top platforms are linked and easy to find. So, your LinkedIn should lead to your site, and your site should have links to your podcast, YouTube channel, or wherever you create the most. You should have all of it buttoned up because the easier it is to find, the more control you have over how people perceive you.

And don't forget the basics. SEO is not just for big blogs; it matters for your name, too. Make sure your site ranks when people type it in. Add some niche-specific keywords, like industry terms, your city, and your title. All of that helps shape what shows up and pushes old or irrelevant stuff down the page.

Your digital authority stack should be intentional. Books, podcasts, media features, speaking gigs, awards, whatever you've done, make sure it's visible and linked back to you. That stuff builds layers of credibility and signals that you're not just another profile. You're someone who's been doing the work and has results to show for it.

The key is to create content that ranks, that's linked to your site, and that tells your story in your words. When people start googling you and they see that consistent narrative across multiple platforms, that's what makes you look like an icon, not just someone saying they are one. Curate what they see and feel when they find you, like the tone, the photos, and the headlines. It should all feel aligned, like it's part of a bigger story you're telling about your work and mission. You might not control the algorithm, but you can absolutely influence the narrative.

Your 12-Month Icon Roadmap—How to Execute Everything in This Book

Alright, so let's talk about how to actually execute everything in this book—not just read it, not just highlight it, but *build it* and turn this whole icon status thing into your reality. I like to break it into a 12-month roadmap, super simple, with four quarters and four big focus areas. If you lock in on these, you'll be unrecognizable a year from now in the best way possible.

Months one through three are all about your foundation. This is where you identify your signature framework, your method, your thing. It doesn't have to be fancy, but it needs to be yours. What's your process, your philosophy, your approach? Start shaping that into an authority asset like a book, a podcast, or stage content, something long form that shows the world how you think and positions you as the expert, not just a service provider.

Months four to six are "go time." Now you're launching your visibility platform. Maybe that's a certification, maybe it's an industry award, maybe it's your first event, or maybe it's just you getting strategic about media. Whatever it is, this is where you go from just talking about what you do to *owning* space in people's minds. You're no longer participating in the conversation; you're leading it.

Months seven to nine are when you bring in systems. This is where you scale with automation. Build your visibility engine using tools like GoHighLevel to schedule content email sequences and text campaigns, and Skool if you're running a community or course platform. Get your backend tight so the front end doesn't drain you. You want this thing running even when you're offline.

Months ten through twelve are the collaboration phase. Now you start partnering up. Find other icons, experts, and thought leaders in your space and build together, whether that's podcast swaps, joint offers, bundles, or giveaways. The goal is to borrow trust from each other's audiences and rise faster together.

To recap your **12-Month Icon Roadmap:**

Months 1–3: Build Your Foundation

- Identify your **signature framework**, method, or unique approach.

- Define your **process, philosophy, or perspective.**

- Begin creating an **authority asset**—such as a book, podcast, or stage talk—to showcase your expertise and elevate you from *service provider* to *thought leader.*

Months 4–6: Launch Your Visibility Platform

- Step into the spotlight with something visible and strategic:
  - Launch a **certification**, win an **industry award**, host your **first event**, or ramp up **media appearances.**

- The goal is to go from just **talking about what you do** to **owning your space** in the industry conversation.

Months 7–9: Scale with Systems

- Bring in **automation and backend systems:**
  - Use tools like **GoHighLevel** for content scheduling, email sequences, and text campaigns.
  - Use **Skool** if running a community or course.

- Create a **self-sustaining visibility engine** that works even when you're offline.

Months 10–12: Collaborate and Expand

- Start **partnering** with other icons, experts, and thought leaders:
  - Do **podcast swaps, joint offers, bundles,** or **giveaways.**

- Leverage each other's audiences to **borrow trust** and **accelerate growth** together.

You're building brand equity through alignment throughout the whole year. You want to set quarterly goals around visibility, not just revenue, but things like how many podcast appearances, how many features, how many speaking gigs, and how many awards. Track the reps so you know you're making moves even when results take time. Set up a simple dashboard, nothing fancy, just a sheet where you track content reach, referrals, Google search traffic—whatever helps you see your authority growing in real time. Then do a quick icon audit every month. Check-in on what's aligned and what's falling flat and adjust accordingly.

The biggest shift here is focusing on compounding visibility, not spikes. You're not chasing virality; you're building a body of work that shows up and stacks over time. The real flex is when someone finds you six months from now and your brand still feels alive, clear, and undeniable.

The Final Challenge—Take Action or Stay Invisible

You can have the best ideas in the world, the most value, the most heart, and the most experience, but if you're not *showing up*, none of it matters. No one's coming to tap you on the shoulder and say, "Hey, you're an icon." It's up to *you* to decide to step into that and start acting like it.

It's never going to feel like the perfect time. No one ever feels totally ready, and if you wait for that moment, it's not going to come. You build this thing as you go. You figure it out on the way up. You get sharper by moving, not by thinking about moving.

The only thing that actually separates the people who are seen and heard from the ones still stuck behind the scenes is action. That's it. Inaction is a fast track to irrelevance. In this world, where everything is moving fast and attention is currency, if you're not actively creating, you're disappearing, and I don't say that to scare you. I say it because once you realize that the power's in your hands, you stop waiting for permission and start creating your own momentum.

You've got the playbook, and you've got the framework, the tech, the tools, and the strategy. It's all here. You know what to do; now it just comes down to whether you'll do it. Yeah, it might be messy at first, and yeah, you might feel a little awkward, and yeah, people might not notice right away, but if you stay in motion, they *will* notice because consistency always wins.

Ask yourself, *What legacy do I want to leave in my space? When someone hears my name, what do I want them to feel? What do I want them to associate me with?* Then ask yourself something even deeper: *Will anyone even see that legacy if I don't step up and share it?*

The answer is—probably not. The real flex isn't being the smartest in the room; it's being the one people can find, the one who shows up, the one who makes an impact that actually reaches people and sticks with them. That doesn't happen by accident; that happens by design. The good news is that you've got everything you need to design it.

So, this is it. This is the challenge, the call to action. You've got the blueprint; now it's time to move. The only question left is, are you gonna keep waiting, or are you gonna make yourself impossible to ignore?

THE CHOICE IS YOURS—BE FORGOTTEN OR BE THE ICON

Let's be real. Ninety-nine percent of businesses stay stuck in obscurity, not because they lack a good product and not because they aren't smart, but because they never decided to not only step into the spotlight but own it. They played it safe. They blended in. They waited for permission, applause, or enough experience to finally step up. In doing so, they got passed over by the ones who simply chose to show up and be louder.

Here's the truth. You don't get icon status by accident. You claim it through the platforms you build, the rooms you host, and the people you connect with through content, community, and positioning that says, "I'm not here to fit in. I'm here to stand out."

The Icon Decision—Do You Want to Own Your Industry or Fade Into Irrelevance?

Ask yourself: *Do I want to fade into obscurity and irrelevance, becoming just one more voice in a crowded space, or do I want to own my industry and be the one everyone talks about and trusts?* You don't need millions of followers, and you certainly don't need venture funding. You just need to decide that you're done being optional and start becoming inevitable.

The Final Commitment—Your Roadmap to Icon Status Starts Now

The roadmap to icon status starts now. Every tool is in front of you. We live in an age where you have an abundance of media platforms. You have a community that is just waiting to be curated. You can build your high-value network. Your stage, voice, and message can all be crafted and perfected. The only thing missing in this equation is your commitment.

Hockey legend Wayne Gretzky once said, "You miss 100 percent of the shots you don't take."

Start now. Build the platform. Host the room. Lead the conversations.

Most importantly, become the icon your industry didn't know it was waiting for.

If you don't claim the space, someone else will, and trust me, the world doesn't need more spectators—it needs more ICONS.

THANK YOU FOR READING OUR BOOK!

JOIN OUR COMMUNITY

Just to say thanks for buying and reading our book,
we would like to invite you to our ICON Community!

Scan the QR Code:

We appreciate your interest in our book and value your feedback, as it helps us improve
future versions. We would appreciate it if you could leave your invaluable review on
Amazon.com with your feedback. Thank you!